MY *Angel* DIARY 2014

JENNY SMEDLEY

HAY HOUSE

Carlsbad, California • New York City • London • Sydney
Johannesburg • Vancouver • Hong Kong • New Delhi

****

By the same author
Past Life Angels
Past Life (meditation CD)
Souls Don't Lie
The Tree That Talked
How to Be Happy
Forever Faithful
Supernaturally True
Pets Have Souls Too
Angel Whispers
Soul Angels
Everyday Angels
Pets Are Forever
Angels Please Hear Me
A Year with the Angels
My Angel Diary 2012
An Angel by Your Side
Soul Mates
My Angel Diary 2013
My Dog Diary 2013
My Cat Diary 2013

Personal Notes

Name _____

Address _____

_____

Phone (home) _____

Phone (work) _____

Phone (mobile) _____

Email _____

In case of emergency please contact:

1.   Name:

     Telephone:

     Relationship:

2.   Name:

     Telephone:

     Relationship:

First published and distributed in the United Kingdom by:
Hay House UK Ltd, Astley House, 33 Notting Hill Gate, London W11 3JQ
Tel: +44 (0)20 3675 2450; Fax: +44 (0)20 3675 2451
www.hayhouse.co.uk

Published and distributed in the United States of America by:
Hay House Inc., PO Box 5100, Carlsbad, CA 92018-5100
Tel: (1) 760 431 7695 or (800) 654 5126
Fax: (1) 760 431 6948 or (800) 650 5115
www.hayhouse.com

Published and distributed in Australia by:
Hay House Australia Ltd, 18/36 Ralph St, Alexandria NSW 2015
Tel: (61) 2 9669 4299; Fax: (61) 2 9669 4144
www.hayhouse.com.au

Published and distributed in the Republic of South Africa by:
Hay House SA (Pty) Ltd, PO Box 990, Witkoppen 2068
Tel/Fax: (27) 11 467 8904
www.hayhouse.co.za

Published and distributed in India by:
Hay House Publishers India, Muskaan Complex, Plot No.3, B-2,
Vasant Kunj, New Delhi 110 070
Tel: (91) 11 4176 1620; Fax: (91) 11 4176 1630
www.hayhouse.co.in

Distributed in Canada by:
Raincoast, 9050 Shaughnessy St, Vancouver BC V6P 6E5
Tel: (1) 604 323 7100; Fax: (1) 604 323 2600

Text © Jenny Smedley, 2013

The moral rights of the author have been asserted.

A catalogue record for this book is available from the British Library.

ISBN: 978-1-78180-179-6

Contents

ANGEL COMMUNICATION AND ME

For many years I've been communicating with angels, and they've been helping me in my life's path. In a few years I changed, with their help, from an overweight, dissatisfied, apparently talentless depressive into an award-winning songwriter, bestselling author and host of my own TV show. Today I also write columns for five magazines across the world. All of this started when an angel entered my consciousness and triggered a whole new life. Since then my connection to angels has become stronger and stronger, and yet still I often need to make sure I'm really listening!

Towards the end of last year I learned something new. That's not really surprising because we are all here to learn, and because angels bring me new things all the time. But this time I learned that we all have what I now call a 'Doctor Angel'. This is the angel to call on if you are suffering an illness or undergoing surgery, or if you are just very scared of an impending diagnosis. They'll calm and support you through your ordeal and also help you trigger your body's ability to heal itself, sometimes with miraculous results. I'll give you some examples of the kind of healing people have experienced later in this diary.

For me this realization came while I was waiting in trepidation for the results of one of the regular tests that women need to have. I'm sure women reading this will empathize with my situation and understand the worry I experienced when awaiting my results, which I'd been told could take anything from one to three weeks. After nine days I was getting progressively more phobic of the postman, as I expected the envelope containing the results to arrive at any moment. On this particular morning, as I was starting to wake up, I heard a voice as clear as a bell say, 'Your doctor's ear, all right?' I assumed it meant my doctor had heard the test results and that they were fine. I didn't recognize the voice, and could only say that it sounded calm and cool, like a professional.

It took my husband, Tony, to make sense of this episode, as he often does with these things. He said, 'I think it's a message from a guide, telling you that he's "here", not mentioning his "ear."' That was when I realized that everything was all right – and at exactly the same moment as the letter containing the test results dropped onto the mat. It then came to me that we all have an angel or guide 'doctor' who takes care of us in such circumstances. My angel was saying, 'It's all right, your doctor is here (dealing with it).' Sure enough, the letter brought good news.

Trust is something that I have to work to maintain constantly, as do most people who believe in angels. It isn't easy.

A few days later I was on my way to a group I facilitate in Taunton, Somerset, and I was waiting to cross the road at a T-junction. There didn't seem to be traffic coming from any of the three directions, so I walked out into the road. The only word to describe what happened next is 'surreal.' As my balance went forwards in the direction I was moving, something touched my shoulder. Simultaneously, as a car sped around the corner from my right, my balance, which should have dragged my weight forwards, was held in stasis. My arms flapped, and I was bent over as the car passed, at speed, virtually inches beneath my head and shoulders. I thought I was going to fall onto the car, because there was no natural way I could keep my balance long enough for the car to pass. But I hovered there for those split seconds, thinking I was going to be killed or at least severely injured. I should have been more prepared to take aversive action because, only a few days previously, my angels had sent me a dream in which I was hit by a car. Maybe subconsciously I was ready and that's what saved me.

WHY SHOULD I BELIEVE IN ANGELS?

In answer to the question above, literally just as I was writing the introduction about the angel doctor, a message came through to me from 'Susan'. It never fails to amaze me how often this sort of thing happens. The timing of the angels, was, as always, impeccable.

About six years ago I was due to have three operations over a period of two years. The first was to have reconstruction work on both of my feet. As I was lying on the operating table being given a general anaesthetic, I became aware of a sweet-smelling perfume around me – I even mentioned it to the nurse who was attending me.

During the second operation the following year, when I had my thyroid removed, I experienced the same sweet smell of flowery but indeterminable perfume.

Six weeks later I was due to have a total hip replacement. During the night before the operation, I awoke to find a glowing golden figure standing over my legs. It was an outline of the body and head of a being about seven feet tall, who seemed to be made out of a solid, glowing

4

fire. It was like looking into the sun, but it didn't hurt my eyes. The being didn't say anything, but radiated an intense power. I became frightened, so I closed my eyes and recited the Lord's Prayer, and then went back to sleep surprisingly easily.

I stayed asleep until the morning and when I woke up, all my worries about the operation had gone. I had complete faith that Spirit and the angels had answered my fear, and that I would no longer be aware of their comforting presence through the sweet smell of perfume, and I felt that all would be well.

Another message, this time from 'Denise', then came through hot on the heels of the first one. Sometimes angels send their help so quickly that it takes your breath away – when that happens, you just know you're on the right track to please them.

About two years ago I went into hospital for a hysterectomy. After the operation I woke up to find a nurse beside my bed asking if I was all right. This nurse had a distinctive hairstyle that I realized was totally different from any of the other nurses' hairstyles.

The next morning when the usual nurse came into the ward, I thanked her for checking on me. She didn't know what I was talking about, as she had been elsewhere in the hospital at the time I'd had the visit. Even now I can still remember very clearly the mysterious visitor and the lovely feeling I received from her.

SMOKE AND MIRRORS, AND THE POWER OF THE UNIVERSE

It might seem like smoke and mirrors sometimes, but in fact the way the universe works isn't a magic trick. When asking the angels for help, you need to understand that they're bound by the Universal Laws.

Think of the universe as a magnifying mirror, like the ones you can use when putting on your make-up. The universe is law-bound to send you events that will create more of the same energy that you give out – only on a bigger scale. Sadly, this means that if you ask for help when you're in a state of desperation and hopelessness or fear and anguish, you will get back events in your life that create more of those emotions, making you feel worse. So if there are changes you want to make in your life, you'll aid your angels enormously if you can ask for their help in the state of energy you would be in *if those changes had already happened*. The obedient universe will then be compelled to send you events that will create that state of mind – only on a larger scale.

Create the emotion of joy when you speak to your angels for help. Put aside your problems and allow the angels' love for you to fill you with bliss. Then you will receive events that create joy. Remember, your angels love you and want to help you, but the universe is a neutral force and its laws have to be obeyed.

To put this even more simply, the better you can *feel* today, the better tomorrow will *be*.

CHARITY CAN START THE JOURNEY

If you're in doubt about how to transform your energy and find it very difficult to be positive in the face of life's difficulties, I'll tell you one way I've discovered that angels seem to absolutely love – that is, giving to others less fortunate than you. The satisfying emotions you get from doing this help angels command the universe to send you events that make you feel even more satisfaction.

When I wanted to do this, it was tough at first. For a lot of our life together, Tony and I didn't have any spare money. I worried about giving our hard-earned cash to some charities, as I was unsure how much money actually made it into the hands of the people who really needed it. So, when I did have a little cash to spare, I'd go into town and buy a couple of packs of prepared sandwiches to give away. In our market town, there are always a few homeless people around. I didn't want to give them money, preferring instead to give them some food. I never had a bad response from any of them.

Then when I had a bit more to spare, I discovered what I think is the greatest charity opportunity in the world – and it's the greatest for two reasons. First, because every penny you give goes directly to the person you want to give it to – and you even get to choose that person. And second, because sometimes it actually costs you nothing to give the donation as it's actually a loan rather than a gift, so the chances are good that you'll get your money back. The charity is called Kiva, and to quote them:

We envision a world where all people – even in the most remote areas of the globe – hold the power to create opportunity for themselves and others. We believe providing safe, affordable access to capital to those in need helps people create better lives for themselves and their families. Making a loan on Kiva is so simple that you may not realize how much work goes on behind the scenes. Kiva works with microfinance institutions on five continents to provide loans to people without access to traditional banking systems. One hundred percent of your loan is sent to these microfinance institutions, which we call Field Partners, who administer the loans in the field.

Kiva relies on a worldwide network of over 450 volunteers who work with our Field Partners, edit and translate borrower stories, and ensure the smooth operation of countless other Kiva programs. 100 percent of every dollar you lend on Kiva goes directly towards funding loans; Kiva does not take a cut. Furthermore, Kiva does not charge interest to our Field Partners, who administer the loans. Kiva is primarily funded through the support of lenders making optional donations.

(See the Resources section on page 231 for the Kiva website details).

Another painless way to give is through the 'pay it forward' philosophy, which doesn't involve any cash at all. With this, you do an act of kindness for someone and instead of taking a payment, you ask them to 'pay it forward' – in other words, they help someone else in the same way.

It's not money that should 'make the world go round', but favours.

THROUGH THE
MOUTHS OF BABES

Angels love babies. This is because babies are so new and uncluttered, and their energy is pure. So, when trying to connect with angels, let out that inner child in yourself!

As a child you could be happy in a moment. You could sense angels around you and thought it normal. You could create a whole world in your mind, and be happy in it. Yet as you grew up, those whimsical ways were pushed out by the 'need' to fit in with society. Angels don't 'do' high society, and they just want us to impress ourselves, not everyone else. Adults tend to go through most of their lives stressing out about stuff that feels important to them, whereas children spend time looking at a cloud or a butterfly. Adults forget, for most of the time, that the things they get so hot and bothered about, such as money and possessions, only bring a transitory happiness and do not last for ever. Should a loved one suddenly die, all the things they worried about will count for nothing.

Love is the only thing that is really everlasting, and children know that.

I think that's why there's a specific 'Baby Angel'. Mums are always telling me their experiences with this angel, which are similar enough to prove it's real. I was recently sent one that was astounding.

Remy didn't send me a story to begin with – she sent me a photo and it was extraordinary. This photo was a still taken from her son's baby-monitor, which recorded videos. It showed a small boy (her son was about two at the time) sitting in his bed. In each of his arms he cradled the form of a baby. On the bed was the ghostly outline of a woman and standing next to the bed was the tall figure of a man wearing a hat. In all the descriptions I've had of the Baby Angel, he has been a tall man in a hat, so I had no doubt who he was. I suggested to Remy that the babies in her son's arms were siblings who had passed to spirit, and that the woman was the grandmother of these babies. I told Remy that I believed the Baby Angel had brought her son's siblings to visit him, and the spirit woman, through her presence, was assuring Remy that her babies were well cared for. I wasn't really surprised when Remy told me that she had indeed lost two babies. One had been miscarried and the other had died when only a few hours old. She also told me that the children's grandmother had lain on the bed in the same position as in the photo, shortly before she died.

I recently had another message from a very good friend, a medium called Ann. She told me about a client of hers, who had been terribly distressed when she had come for a reading. It turned out that the client had miscarried two babies, one after the other and was deeply traumatized, as many mothers are, by these events. Ann is a clairvoyant (one who sees spirits), and she said that within seconds of the woman entering her cottage, she (Ann) could see a fairy, accompanied by a tall man wearing a hat, standing in front of her. The fairy told Ann that miscarried babies who don't later return to their mother in a new body, become what we would call 'fairies'. She was delighted when I was able confirm what she'd seen because of her description of the Baby Angel. I thought it was a wonderful thing to know that babies who elect not to become humans, instead become fairies. The client was astonished, mostly because she said that since she was a child she had been fascinated by fairies and had collected fairy items, and that even today her house is full of them. Now she knows why.

THE NON-IMPORTANCE OF WORDS

When I was at school people were very fussy about using the right words for everything. The words in the dictionary were available to use and that was it. Nowadays things are very different. The change seemed to start – for me, anyway – in the late 1960s or early 70s, when new words, like 'groovy' for instance, popped up and were adopted. As the years passed by, 'wicked' became 'great', 'sick' became 'wonderful' and everyone started sentences with: 'I was like...'. As a writer, and someone who excelled in English at school, I didn't like all this. I've noticed recently that new words are being used more and more – people just seem to make them up as they go along.

But, I've come to like it. One reason is that you can still always tell what people mean by their words, because more and more they are wearing their emotions on their sleeves. This is a truly wonderful thing. Why? Because angels don't use words at all, they just use energy, or emotion. Yes, of course, you may have 'heard' an angel speak, and I have too, but that's simply because, as humans, we *expect* to hear words. For their own purposes angels don't use names or expressions. They just recognize each other and us by the respective energy states, and communicate through feelings that are far more expressive than words.

We've all had instances when we've misunderstood what someone meant, whether it was in an email or a text, or in speech. But with emotions there are no misunderstandings because if you know how someone feels about you, you know exactly what they mean. As humans, we still have a huge way to go, but by releasing the bonds around words, we're allowing more and more expression and less and less stuffiness. Eventually, I'm sure we'll be as spiritually evolved as angels and we won't need words to communicate. So next time you feel like correcting someone for saying, 'I was like…' instead of 'I did…' or 'I said…' step back and remember that their angels understand them perfectly – maybe better than angels can understand people who create great tracts of prose.

This year, try not to be so 'wordy' and start to rely more on empathy, because having compassion for others and understanding their emotions is the way forward for the world.

ANGEL MEDITATION

The best way to use this is either to record yourself speaking it aloud in a clear, calm voice so that you can play it back to yourself, or to have a friend read it out to you.

Take several deep breaths and, with each one, allow your body to relax from your head down to your toes. Pay particular attention to your jaw and your shoulders, as these areas are where tension begins. Shut your mind to all your cares and worries, and simply concentrate on relaxing your muscles and breathing regularly and deeply. Close your eyes whenever it feels right.

Now visualize a cloud of soft violet mist drifting down from above your head, enveloping your whole body as it passes down over your shoulders, your torso, past your legs and feet. You feel yourself getting more drowsy and relaxed. You look into the swirling mist through your 'third eye' in the centre of your forehead and see the beautiful cloud light up as the sun breaks through.

Next, you imagine a shaft of sunlight in front of you, lighting up a beautiful, perfect, single rose that sits atop a long stem. This rose is a mixture of gentle shades — you've never seen one like it before: pink and peach, apricot and lilac ripple through its satiny petals. As you draw closer to the rose it becomes bigger, so much so that you can climb into it and rest on its downy petals.

Now there's an angel approaching you. He's your own guardian angel and if you observe him carefully, you'll remember his appearance after the meditation. You feel very safe in his company. He's going to bring you many gifts, which he'll place on the ground around your feet.

First he gives you a shield, telling you that this will give you the courage to move forward this year, knowing that you are safe and protected. Next, he brings you a green, glowing ball, which will enable you to be gentle with yourself and others, and will heal your heart from any pain that lingers from last year.

He gives you a quartz crystal containing wisdom and intuition so that you'll understand any messages and dreams that he sends. Now he places next to you an artist's paintbrush to show you that by changing your energy to a feeling of calm and achievement, you really can 'paint' your own future. This brush will help you think of and fill your mind with only the positive things in your life, so that you will receive more and more positive things in return.

He brings you a mirror that will bring clarity to your purpose every day and constantly remind you that you came here with a purpose and a job to do. Next, he *gives you a candle, burning brightly, which will help you to understand the true wonder of your self and all the beauty that surrounds you every day. It will make sure you don't miss any of the small miracles that occur daily.*

He gives you a small diary, which will help you to have a clear and limitless memory to forgive the wrongs you feel have been committed against you, and will bring glimpses of past lives you need to explore and heal. He brings you a small globe, a replica of the Earth, so that you can help to guard and protect her and appreciate what a beautiful home you have while you're human. Lastly, he gives you a sword and a crown. They will help you to be assertive when you need to be, and fair and just when you make decisions and judgements in your everyday life. They will also endow you with the gift of being graceful and generous, whatever the situation.

You see all of these gifts around your feet and know, without doubt, that you can call on your angel at any time, and that you will have his gifts alongside you for ever. Now it's time to say farewell, and you watch as your angel gradually fades and disappears. You arise from your rose bed and, as you do so, imagine the violet mist descending around you again, floating you back gently to normal consciousness and the outside world.

When you are ready, you slowly open your eyes. You are feeling very calm and relaxed, safe in the knowledge that all the gifts your angel gave you are ready for you to use whenever you need them.

THE YEAR AHEAD

You've now gone through uncertainty and worry relating to global concerns in the press about the 'end of the world' according to the Mayan Calendar in December 2012, and perhaps felt the unsettling effects that such events brought in 2013. But, happily, 2014 is going to bring welcome respite. People everywhere are becoming more truthful, more honest about the way the world is run so unfairly by a privileged few, and humanity will become more compassionate as a result.

This is all to do with the spiritual ascension we've been moving towards since the end of 2012. Of course, it will be an on-going, gradual process to bring equality and give all humans and animals their rights, but we will make good progress this year. Finances, too, won't be so difficult to balance, as a more natural order will evolve when people start to realize that money doesn't make them happy. Real happiness – the kind that is generated from 'within' rather than dependent on events and possessions from 'without' – comes from a deep sense of fulfillment which, in turn, comes from finding and following one's true path.

To see the truth in this you only have to watch the reality TV shows in which celebrities live for a short time in a hostile environment and have to earn their food and privileges. The stars of these shows usually start off by bemoaning the luxuries they are missing, but very soon their priorities change. They begin to get hungry, and as food dominates their minds they start to think like team players, they learn tolerance for their fellow contestants and develop true empathy – feelings that they may have long buried. You'll often see a complete switch in them as they start to recognize what's actually important in their lives and what they need to be truly happy.

So this year, concentrate on your real priorities. Recognize when they change and make adjustments in your life to follow them. This sounds simple, but so many of us seem unwilling or too afraid to make changes, and we remain stuck and blunder onwards regardless, often ending up sad and frustrated.

So, if your angels put thoughts of what you should be doing and focusing upon into your head, especially in 2014, listen and be brave.

Finally, a special thank you to my Facebook fans for suggesting the weekly angel-inspired quotes (denoted with a 💬 symbol) that appear on the pages of this year's diary.

Weekly Diary

2014

JANUARY

M	T	W	T	F	S	S
		1	2	3	4	5
6	7	8	9	10	11	12
13	14	15	16	17	18	19
20	21	22	23	24	25	26
27	28	29	30	31		

FEBRUARY

M	T	W	T	F	S	S
					1	2
3	4	5	6	7	8	9
10	11	12	13	14	15	16
17	18	19	20	21	22	23
24	25	26	27	28		

MARCH

M	T	W	T	F	S	S
31					1	2
3	4	5	6	7	8	9
10	11	12	13	14	15	16
17	18	19	20	21	22	23
24	25	26	27	28	29	30

APRIL

M	T	W	T	F	S	S
	1	2	3	4	5	6
7	8	9	10	11	12	13
14	15	16	17	18	19	20
21	22	23	24	25	26	27
28	29	30				

MAY

M	T	W	T	F	S	S
		1	2	3	4	
5	6	7	8	9	10	11
12	13	14	15	16	17	18
19	20	21	22	23	24	25
26	27	28	29	30	31	

JUNE

M	T	W	T	F	S	S
30						1
2	3	4	5	6	7	8
9	10	11	12	13	14	15
16	17	18	19	20	21	22
23	24	25	26	27	28	29

JULY

M	T	W	T	F	S	S
	1	2	3	4	5	6
7	8	9	10	11	12	13
14	15	16	17	18	19	20
21	22	23	24	25	26	27
28	29	30	31			

AUGUST

M	T	W	T	F	S	S
				1	2	3
4	5	6	7	8	9	10
11	12	13	14	15	16	17
18	19	20	21	22	23	24
25	26	27	28	29	30	31

SEPTEMBER

M	T	W	T	F	S	S
1	2	3	4	5	6	7
8	9	10	11	12	13	14
15	16	17	18	19	20	21
22	23	24	25	26	27	28
29	30					

OCTOBER

M	T	W	T	F	S	S
		1	2	3	4	5
6	7	8	9	10	11	12
13	14	15	16	17	18	19
20	21	22	23	24	25	26
27	28	29	30	31		

NOVEMBER

M	T	W	T	F	S	S
					1	2
3	4	5	6	7	8	9
10	11	12	13	14	15	16
17	18	19	20	21	22	23
24	25	26	27	28	29	30

DECEMBER

M	T	W	T	F	S	S
1	2	3	4	5	6	7
8	9	10	11	12	13	14
15	16	17	18	19	20	21
22	23	24	25	26	27	28
29	30	31				

January

Start this year with a better sense of who you are and what you're here for. It's hard sometimes to believe that another whole year has passed since last January, but it has, so try and experience every moment fully. Remember the saying, 'This, too, shall pass', because everything passes quickly, good or bad. So appreciate the difference and enjoy each moment of bliss for as long as possible. Living in the moment can help you to focus in on your life path and move forward with a positive spirit into the year of 2014. Shake off all those old patterns that have pushed you down for the last twelve months and start anew with fresh, confident determination.

WHAT SHOULD YOU FOCUS ON?

This month is the ideal time to hone and develop your creative skills, especially when it comes to creating your new reality. Whatever you've been moaning about in your life up till now, this is the time to take action. Don't sit around and wait any longer for things to come to you, because if all you do is wish, then all you'll ever be doing is wishing. If you do what you always did, you'll get what you always got. Rather, make positive plans to bring the things you desire into your life. Make a list of everything you need and want, and start acting as if you already have them. For instance if you yearn for more financial security, stop creeping around the charity shops, afraid to look at prices in up-market stores. Instead go window-shopping in those expensive places and concentrate on having the air of someone who can afford the things they sell. This is what successful people do – and it works! If you want a new job or relationship, try as much as possible to 'feel' as if you already have one, and in time reality will come to match your emotions.

PLANET OF THE MONTH – CERES

This body, which is the size of Texas, started off being classified as an asteroid when it was discovered in 1801. But the rules were changed and in 2006 it became accepted as a dwarf planet. So what better way to start this new beginning for you at this time of year than by focusing on the meaning of a new planet? Ceres represents the natural world and celebrates the bond between a parent and their child. It is a symbol of birth, death, re-birth and new beginnings. Ceres helps to prepare us for regeneration in the coming year. Like our crops and the plants and trees that surround us, we have been placed on the planet to learn and grow, live and die and then come back in the form of seeds to continue our lessons and develop accordingly. Ceres can teach us that our death is not the end, and just as last year has been reborn into this one, so we, too, will be reborn. Use Ceres as a focus to energize yourself for another year and be more determined than ever to change your life for the better.

ANGIE'S STORY

I'm starting the year with Angie's amazing story. It shows that with a good heart and compassion for others, we can bring help from our angels in times of distress and hopelessness, and often from unexpected quarters.

I went on holiday to Greece when I was in my 20s, and decided to stay on afterwards with my friend and work there for the summer. This friend turned out not to be a good choice and caused me all sorts of trouble, including a horrible experience involving a sexual assault. Then my boyfriend at the time came over to Greece and ended our relationship. I had no money to get home... you get the picture... I realized that this place was not right for me. Sure, I could have rung home and got someone to buy me a ticket, but I felt compelled to move on to the next island.

This was a completely different place to the mainland and mostly non-commercial. There were a lot of artists around there and Greek families with holiday homes. I discovered my ex-boyfriend working in a moped hire place, and for short while we got back together, so I thought that was why I'd felt compelled to go to this island. However, after a while things got nasty and I ended up sitting in the village square crying my eyes out and spending my last drachma on waffles and chocolate sauce!

I was feeling so alone and desolate and then I heard a voice saying, "Don't worry, I am sending you help." I really thought I must have imagined it, but was comforted by it anyway, and then I saw two gorgeous young Greek men approaching me. They said, "Here she is... our angel." I thought, how bizarre, but also my 'gaydar' went off overtime around them, so I felt no sexual threat from them.

I told them about my situation and they invited me to stay with them. I know it sounds illogical to trust strangers like that but I really just knew they wouldn't harm me. We became great friends and they soon admitted that they were in a relationship together and that one of their fathers had found out and tried to beat it out of him. This was their last summer before going to do National Service, and of course they really wanted to be together, and being very spiritual people, they had prayed to their angels for someone to help them. They saw me straight away — with my white blonde hair, crying into my waffle, they just knew I'd been sent to help!

We hatched a plan where I pretended to be a girlfriend to one of them and this kept the father off their back, as he was happy to think that his red-blooded son had just gone through a strange phase and was now 'normal'! We had a fantastic summer and I kept in touch with them both for many years.

I feel that angels sent those guys into my path to renew my faith in people, especially men, as they were both so kind and protective, showing me how men could be. Their presence helped me to stop the pattern of inviting *not-so-nice men into my life, so that things would work out right for me. Soon after that I met my now husband, and we've now been happily married 16 years.*

ANGELS IN THE NEWS

Brian, a 3 year-old boy in the USA, got trapped under an automatic garage door. He'd been there long enough for paramedics to think him dead and not believe he could be revived. The door had closed right over his heart, stopping it. However Brian was successfully brought back to life and a while afterwards Brian said to his mother, "Do you remember when I got stuck under the garage door? Well, it was so heavy and it hurt real bad. I called to you, but you couldn't hear me. I started to cry, but then it hurt too bad. And then the 'birdies' came. The birdies made a whooshing sound and flew into the garage. They took care of me. One of the birdies came and got you. She came to tell you I got stuck under the door."

ANGEL SYMBOL FOR JANUARY

This month look for small items of jewellery with an angel on them, such as the 'angel on my shoulder' pin.

DEC/JAN 2014 *Week 1*

30 Monday

31 Tuesday

'Angel love and light surrounds me at all times... for ever.'
Ruthie Young

1 Wednesday ●

2 Thursday

This week's angel-inspired word is PARADISE ★

3 Friday

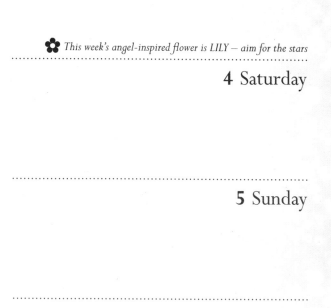

🌼 *This week's angel-inspired flower is LILY — aim for the stars*

4 Saturday

5 Sunday

♥ *Angel lesson*

A state of nirvana is really available if you choose to trust.

JANUARY 2014 *Week 2*

6 Monday

This week's angel-inspired words are BE REAL ★

7 Tuesday

8 Wednesday ☽

This week's angel-inspired flower is SNOWDROP — have hope ✿

9 Thursday

10 Friday

11 Saturday

'That cool breeze could just be an angel kiss.' Christina Christou

12 Sunday

💜 *Angel lesson*
Never pretend to yourself.

JANUARY 2014 *Week 3*

13 Monday

14 Tuesday

'Angels hear you even when your plea for help is whispered'
Lynn Kilpatrick

15 Wednesday

16 Thursday ○

This week's angel-inspired flower is WITCH HAZEL — expect magical events to unfold. ✿

17 Friday

★ *This week's angel-inspired word is OBSERVE*

18 Saturday

19 Sunday

♥ *Angel lesson*
Never miss a moment of beauty.

JANUARY 2014 *Week 4*

···

20 Monday

This week's angel-inspired flower is ZINNIA — be joyful and joy will come to you ✿

···

21 Tuesday

···

22 Wednesday

'Love is the presence of an angel.' Moira Fitzsimmons 💬

···

23 Thursday

···

◑ 24 Friday

25 Saturday

★ *This week's angel-inspired word is FULFILMENT*

26 Sunday

 *Angel lesson*

Achieving your angel's wishes for you brings happiness to you faster than your own wishes can.

JANUARY 2014 *Week 5*

27 Monday

28 Tuesday

This week's angel-inspired word is HONESTY ★

29 Wednesday

30 Thursday ●

This week's angel-inspired flower is CAMELLIA — you are worthy of being loved

31 Friday

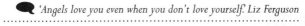 *'Angels love you even when you don't love yourself.'* Liz Ferguson

1 Saturday

2 Sunday

*Pagan festival of Imbolc: a celebration of the sun's gradual return.
We note the first daffodils pushing up into the light.
It's a time of rebirth, of our sun and of ourselves.*

 *Angel lesson*

Thank your angel every day — we all like to be appreciated.

February

The dull and often cold days of February can make time drag. So, concentrate on the things you can work on indoors, in the warm. If you start to feel a bit stir-crazy, then get yourself a dog, which will be great at forcing you outside for a bracing walk. It feels wonderful to know that you've 'done your duty' and you're free to cuddle up in the warm for the rest of the day without a guilty conscience. This is also a great frame of mind in which to hear the words of your guides and angels while everything inside is peaceful and still and outside the weather rages. Try meditating by gazing into an open fire or the heart of a candle flame.

WHAT SHOULD YOU FOCUS ON?

By now you're starting to recover from the over-indulgence of the holiday season and your body needs exercise and a good diet to build it up for the year to come. If you don't get healthy and don't top up the 'sunshine vitamin,' (vitamin D), it's easy to let a sense of anti-climax and the realization that there's more winter to come, bring your spirits down. Don't just concentrate on your physical body though – also think about how your chakras (energy centres) may have become blocked and stagnant. If your chakras are blocked you won't be inviting angels in to help you.

PLANET OF THE MONTH – ERIS

Eris was discovered in 2005 and has been designated a dwarf planet. In Greek mythology Eris was the goddess of the night and dark feelings. We're all capable of releasing the 'Eris' in us, when we feel vengeful or angry and want to seek retribution. These are the emotions we need to focus on controlling and releasing during the month of February. Becoming refreshed and renewed is our aim, so that this year can bring novel and wonderful experiences. It's no good stifling such emotions though, because if that's all we do they will find a way to break through. What we need to do when we try to halt these feelings is to turn our minds to something else entirely – spend your time making positive plans for the year ahead instead. The more you focus on them, the more you will make them happen.

JASON'S STORY
Jason's story shows how to deal with a really negative situation.

I was homeless, scared, broke and alone. I didn't really know what to do in the night when the city shut down, and I spent my days anywhere I could be comfortable for free, like parks, libraries, McDonald's – if I felt like splurging. At night it got more difficult. And by this time it had been going on for months. One day I sat alone, homeless in Queen's Park, clipping my nails and trying to feel like a dignified, worthwhile human being. I'd only eaten a single muffin and a single croissant in three days. I felt pretty broken; beaten up by life.

I had big dreams, big ambitions, and here I was miles away from them all with no one I felt I could turn to. I was letting my thoughts run away with me when suddenly, an old man approached me, and in a thick accent he asked, "Are you homeless?"

Tenaciously holding on to any shred of dignity I could muster, I replied, "No, I'm just chillin' ".

He looked at me briefly, cocked his head and then said, "Well, my friend over there…" He gestured to an even older man, sitting on a bench… "wants you to have this." He then handed me an Ambrose's Organics (a natural food store) bag.

What else could I do but take it? I opened it and glanced in quickly. Inside was a piping hot loaf of freshly baked bread, a banana and a new, unopened bottle of water. I thanked the man and he wandered off. The whole experience was absolutely surreal, and I could feel some electric, magnetic charge in the air as it all went down. That food kept me full for about two days. I never saw the men again. Did I suddenly feel blessed, cared for by life and that I was worth something to someone, somewhere? Yes, I sure did.

JASMINE'S STORY

I'm of a faith where I'm not allowed to believe in what I choose, and I thought that angels wouldn't protect me because of that. I was so afraid all the time, but not now.

I was going up a steep flight of stone stairs near my home and I didn't notice that someone had spilled cooking oil on them. My foot slipped and I went over backwards. My head hit one step and I tumbled over and over, unable to stop. At one point my body actually took flight, and I knew that when I landed at the bottom of the steps I would be knocked out, and almost certainly have broken some bones.

Suddenly a pair of arms snatched me out of the air. They were so real that I assumed a man had been standing on the steps and had caught me as I flew past him. I clung to the strong body and he placed me on the ground. I was dizzy but I looked up to thank him, embarrassed at having been held so close by a strange man. There was no one there. No one on the steps, no one on the street below, and nowhere the man could have gone.

Apart from a few bruises and a sore head I was completely unhurt. I just know it was an angel who saved me, and that I am protected even if my beliefs have to remain a secret.

ANGELS IN THE NEWS
A CCTV camera in Cilandak Town Square in Jakarta, Indonesia, took a remarkable film one night. It shows a winged being, made of light, land and then take off again. So that you can judge for yourself, I've listed the link in the Resources section at the back of the diary.

ANGEL SYMBOL FOR FEBRUARY
Sometimes a special scent, usually of a flower, will let you know your angel is near but it can also be something that might seem odd, like tobacco.

31 Friday

 'Angels love you even when you don't love yourself.' Liz Ferguson

1 Saturday

2 Sunday

Pagan festival of Imbolc: a celebration of the sun's gradual return.
We note the first daffodils pushing up into the light.
It's a time of rebirth, of our sun and of ourselves.

♥ *Angel lesson*

Thank your angel every day — we all like to be appreciated.

FEBRUARY 2014 *Week 6*

3 Monday

*This week's angel-inspired flower is ANTHURIUM — welcome new
friends into your life* ❀

4 Tuesday

5 Wednesday

'My Heavenly companion is never more than a thought away.' 💬
Mary McShane

6 Thursday ◗

7 Friday

8 Saturday

★ *This week's angel-inspired word is VARIETY*

9 Sunday

♥ *Angel lesson*
Embrace racial differences and celebrate diversity.

FEBRUARY 2014 *Week 7*

10 Monday

....

11 Tuesday

This week's angel-inspired word is BROADEN ★
....

12 Wednesday

....

13 Thursday

'The angels' love for you makes you shine like a beacon.'
Lynn Kilpatrick
....

○ **14** Friday

✿ *This week's angel-inspired flower is CROCUS*
— be happy, no matter what

15 Saturday

16 Sunday

♥ *Angel lesson*
There are no limits when angel wings lift you.

FEBRUARY 2014 *Week 8*

17 Monday

18 Tuesday

This week's angel-inspired flower is HOLLYHOCK — be confident, you can do it! ✿

19 Wednesday

20 Thursday

21 Friday

'On angels' wings, we glide on the tides of love.' Simon Oliver

◑ **22** Saturday

23 Sunday

★ This week's angel-inspired word is ADMIRATION

♥ *Angel lesson*
Look on your angel and let love fill your heart.

FEBRUARY 2014 *Week 9*

....

24 Monday

....

25 Tuesday

*This week's angel-inspired flower is PETUNIA — meditate with
your angel* ❁
....

26 Wednesday

....

27 Thursday

'A life led by angels = a life filled with love.' Silverla StMichael 💬
....

28 Friday

★ *This week's angel-inspired word is CONSIDER*

 1 Saturday

2 Sunday

♥ *Angel lesson*
Each word you say has an effect on someone, so be careful.

March

March is a strange month. It's neither winter nor spring.
It can behave like a lion or a lamb and often leaves us
not knowing what to wear or where to go, making plans
pretty much impossible. So, this is a month to go with
the flow and keep trust and faith alive when life spins us
up and down. This time should also be used to rediscover
your compassion for fellow human beings, because it's
all too easy to lose this without realizing. Tragedies are
constantly thrown in our faces, so during this month,
whenever possible avoid watching the TV news, don't
open newspapers and, instead, try to rekindle the
sympathetic feelings you used to have when you heard
of others' misfortunes.

WHAT SHOULD YOU FOCUS ON?

This is the month to focus on resolving conflicts, especially long-standing ones. Any arguments that prey on your mind create the wrong kind of energy. The state of your energy is paramount in connecting with angels, and little niggles can prevent the energy being right. March brings about the faint beginnings of spring, the time when buds start to swell, and the health of those buds denotes the strength of the harvest many months down the road. It's the same for your year – you need the seeds of relationships to be strong and pure and not polluted.

PLANET OF THE MONTH – MARS

As March is named after the Roman god Mars, the planet of the same name is the obvious choice for this month. Mars is often thought of as the god of war, but originally he was seen as a military seeker of peace and this is why it's a time to make peace and bury old arguments, not to fight. You'll need to do it now because Mars often generates cycles that you may tend to keep going through with certain people. So any old angst that you allow to linger will quickly grow at this time, just as new shoots do. Break the cycle and use the focus of the fiery red planet to light up your shadows and expose things the way they really are. This will help you admit to yourself when it's *you* who's making mistakes in relationships. If this all means that you have to eat some humble pie, do it, knowing that it's for your own good in the end.

VJ'S STORY

This story shows how you can find courage in the face of life's ups and downs and how angels shower little miracles on you, if you have enough trust.

In 1987, I was 32 years old and was diagnosed with breast cancer. My surgeon said a radical, total mastectomy was my only option. His verdict was that the tumour was large and he had seen smaller tumours from which women had died.

I went into a bookstore looking for information and overheard a woman telling the clerk that she wanted to work with cancer patients on visualization. I told her that I wasn't sure if I was going to survive this cancer or not, and she said she would support me whatever happened.

Two days before my surgery, she was guiding me through a visualization in which the intent was for the best possible surgical outcome. I had a vision of my guardian angel sitting next to me and I was told that I would not die from this cancer and I did not have to be deformed. I was shown a more limited type of surgery.

The next day in the pre-op meeting with my surgeon, I 'negotiated' over what he could and could not do – he told me that what I was asking was impossible. Yet I stood firm against his medical objections. The team did a new type of surgery – a quadectomy – in which they removed a quarter of my breast (I'm in medical books). When the bandages were removed, my breast looked exactly how I had been shown by the angel. And 25 years later, I'm still alive.

JUNE'S STORY

It was June 2010 and I'd arranged to meet a male friend I'd known for a long time. As we came to the end of the afternoon we agreed it would be best, for various, difficult reasons, if we didn't keep in contact, although it made us very sad. So with heavy hearts and a few tears we said our final goodbyes.

The weeks that followed were heart-wrenching, as I missed my friend so much, and I cast around for ways to connect in a small way without breaking any promises. I asked a female friend if she would go to see a clairvoyant with me to see if she could up with anything, and we made appointment for late August.

On the day of the appointment it was a very sunny day, so I waited outside for my friend to pick me up. While I was waiting I closed my eyes and with every ounce of strength I had in me, I asked the angels whether my male friend missed and thought about me as much as I missed and thought about him. I asked them to send me a brightly coloured bird, such as a parrot, as a sign. I opened my eyes and looked up at the sky and smiled to myself – was I expecting to see a parrot fly by?

At that point my female friend drove up and we set off on our journey. We'd been driving for about 35 minutes when we pulled off the motorway, where we hit very slow moving traffic. I looked at the car in front and turned to my friend, asking, "What's that in the car in front of us?" Just as I said that the driver in front opened his window and perched a very brightly coloured, live parrot on the wing mirror. My friend laughed at this very rare sight, while I thanked the angels very quietly from the bottom of my heart.

ANGELS IN THE NEWS

A camera in Mecca, Arabia captured something strange landing on the roof of the Kaaba, the most sacred Islamic building. I've listed the link to the film in the Resources section so that you can judge for yourself whether or not it was an angel.

ANGEL SYMBOL FOR MARCH

Shapes in the clouds are the images to look for this month, as the clouds at this time are spectacular. The shape you see will represent something new coming into your life.

....

28 Friday

⭐ *This week's angel-inspired word is CONSIDER*
....

● **1** Saturday

....

2 Sunday

....

♥ *Angel lesson*

Each word you say has an effect on someone, so be careful.

MARCH 2014 *Week 10*

....

3 Monday

This week's angel-inspired flower is DAHLIA —
be elegant in what you say ❀
....

4 Tuesday

....

5 Wednesday

'Stay positive, talk to your angels every day, give thanks.' 🗨
Hazel Chubb
....

6 Thursday

....

7 Friday

 8 Saturday

★ *This week's angel-inspired word is COMPANION*

9 Sunday

♥ *Angel lesson*

Friends come in all shapes and sizes, so treasure every single one.

MARCH 2014 *Week 11*

10 Monday

11 Tuesday

'The simplest magick is angel magick — tell them your dreams.'
Silverla StMichael

12 Wednesday

13 Thursday

This week's angel-inspired words are LET GO ★

14 Friday

This week's angel-inspired flower is BORAGE — have courage

15 Saturday

○ **16** Sunday

Angel lesson

*Become free from the constraints that society
puts on you and follow your dreams.*

MARCH 2014 *Week 12*

17 Monday

18 Tuesday

This week's angel-inspired flower is ASTER — trust ✿

19 Wednesday

20 Thursday

Pagan festival of Ostara: thanksgiving for the return of life and the start of a brand new cycle. Easter bunnies and chocolate eggs are taken from the two Pagan symbols of this time: rabbits and eggs.

21 Friday

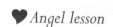 *'Live and love life, and trust your angels.'* Rosemarie Robinson

22 Saturday

★ *This week's angel-inspired words are BE FLEXIBLE*

23 Sunday

♥ *Angel lesson*

Allow your angel to take you out of your comfort zone so that you can develop further than you ever thought possible.

MARCH 2014 *Week 13*

24 Monday ☽

....

25 Tuesday

This week's angel-inspired flower is BIRD OF PARADISE — accept your magnificence ✿
....

26 Wednesday

....

27 Thursday

'My angels always remind me that I matter.' Christina Christou 💬
....

28 Friday

 ★ *This week's angel-inspired word is CONFIDENCE*

29 Saturday

● **30** Sunday

♥ *Angel lesson*

Step forward into each day, assured that your angel will do what's best for you.

MARCH/APR 2014 *Week 14*

31 Monday

This week's angel-inspired word is LINGER ★

1 Tuesday

2 Wednesday

This week's angel-inspired flower is PASSION FLOWER – stay calm ❀

3 Thursday

April

At this point in springtime you need to operate at as high a vibration as possible. Right now our planet Earth and the plants and animals on it are at the peak of their energy, so to be in tune with them and the home we all share, you need to be at the peak of your energy, too. One way to do this is to clear all your clutter, both mental and physical. Be ruthless. If someone constantly upsets and angers you, maybe this is the time to cut them loose to follow their own path, without them interfering with yours. If you have clothes and possessions you haven't used for two years or more, donate them to charity. You'll feel better for it.

WHAT SHOULD YOU FOCUS ON?

Clearing space for new ideas and things will help you feel less attracted to media such as TV, newspapers and magazines and you won't find yourself relying on them for relaxation. Because of this you'll also become less dependent on things like alcohol, tranquilizers and so on. These dependencies are one of the 'easy-fix' curses of the modern world, which of course are not really permanent fixes at all. Without them you'll become instantly healthier, too, which will remove 'brain fog', and help your mind's processes to work more efficiently. One thing you'll discover is that you are more able to create your own serenity. Creativity of all kinds is often blocked when information overload literally clogs up your imagination. Your inner memory 'filing cabinet' gets so huge that you can't find your way around it. Give your mind some space, stop filling it with random and useless chatter and little by little your inventive brain will think of new and positive things to occupy itself.

PLANET OF THE MONTH – NEPTUNE

Neptune can help to set you free from the constraints and everyday clutter of the conscious mind. This is essential for lifting your vibration to a more spiritual level, and facilitating your communication with your higher self and your angels. It can also increase your intuition, which is a natural result from raising your vibration. This will help you to shake off the shackles of any possession-envy that might still linger in your spirit, and which, if allowed to continue, would chain you to harmful thought cycles and prevent you creating a wonderful new reality. You get what you ask for, so, by thinking envious thoughts, all you will ever receive is material possessions which will never fulfill you, only leave you full of emptiness.

The influence of Neptune will also take away any tendency to be too independent, allowing a closer connection to all those of high value to your spiritual lifestyle, and preventing you from shutting yourself off. From there you will feel a greater ability to generate the visionary process while avoiding anything that is solely of surface value and is pure escapism.

RUSTY'S STORY

This is a great account of how angels can change your life if you become open enough.

My mother ran a gift store in Florida and she'd been praying for some information on how to be an effective witness to people of the Jewish faith without being offensive to them.

One afternoon, the door opened, and a young man with a backpack came in. Mother looked up surprised and said, "I didn't see you come across the sidewalk or the parking lot, how did you get here?"

In answer he just laid his backpack on the counter, took out some papers and handed them to her, saying, "I was told you needed this." My mother saw that it was the information she'd prayed about. She was amazed and invited him to church with us the next day, Sunday, and he agreed to meet us there. He turned to leave as the telephone rang. Mother picked it up. When she looked back up the man had vanished. She went outside to look for him so she could thank him properly but he was nowhere in sight.

On Sunday at church, Mother looked over her shoulder and on the very last pew was the young man with a female companion. Mother went back and spoke to them, shook their hands and welcomed them to the service and invited them to join us at home for lunch. She told my dad they were in the rear of the church, and he saw them. He waved and they waved back. At the end of the service the Pastor shook everyone's hand as they were leaving, but there was no sign of the couple. The Pastor said he'd seen them sitting in the pew and they hadn't come out, but they were gone. This mystery was discussed among our family for years as Mother thought they were angels.

Years later, I returned to that same church and was dining with the Pastor and his wife, when I brought up my mother's angel story. The Pastor then told me the rest of the story that my parents didn't know. He said, "Sometime after you moved away, I was preaching on Sunday night. I looked in the back of the church and there sat a young man I thought I'd seen before, but I wasn't sure. At the end I asked anyone who wished to accept Christ as their Saviour to come down and be baptized, and the young man did. We went to the baptismal room to change clothes. The young man changed into a blue robe in the presence of two ushers, then he ascended the stairs, walked into the water, was baptized and then walked out."

The pastor continued, "After I had baptized a young lady, I left the water and went down the stairs to where the two ushers were. I asked them where the young man was. And they looked at me as if I was joking. They said he had never come down the stairs. Then I remembered where I'd seen him before. It was that time your mother invited him to church — the same man. I baptized an Angel!"

SAM'S STORY

This is short but a wonderful symbol.

Years ago, when I was only 16, I felt I couldn't go on any more because I was being bullied. I hadn't told my parents how bad I felt. One night I was sitting on my *bed, and was seriously contemplating ending my life, when suddenly I felt a pair of arms wrap right around me and hug me. I wasn't at all afraid as you might expect. It lasted about ten minutes. The next morning I walked differently, had a different energy, and I was able to ignore the bullies. And after a couple of weeks they left me alone — all because I knew I had a guardian angel with me.*

ANGELS IN THE NEWS

In 2009 geologist Dr. Morris Charles claimed that NASA lab workers had found a carving of an angel in one of the rocks brought to Earth by the Apollo 11 astronauts in 1969. Dr. Charles was a NASA scientist for 23 years. I have put the link in the Resources section at the end of the diary.

ANGEL SYMBOL FOR APRIL

Sensations of a gentle touch on the shoulder or a soft breeze when there is none, ruffling your hair. This symbol will tell you that your angel is always there to comfort you.

MARCH/APR 2014 *Week 14*

31 Monday

This week's angel-inspired word is LINGER ⭐

1 Tuesday

2 Wednesday

This week's angel-inspired flower is PASSION FLOWER –
stay calm 🌼

3 Thursday

4 Friday

5 Saturday

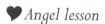 *'Let angels show you the silver lining of the clouds.'*
Lynn Kilpatrick

6 Sunday

♥ *Angel lesson*

Don't be in such a hurry. Angels have all the
time in the universe for you.

APRIL 2014 *Week 15*

7 Monday ☽

8 Tuesday

This week's angel-inspired flower is FORSYTHIA — expect excitement ✿

9 Wednesday

10 Thursday

'Trust in your angels, then let it go. Expect miracles to appear!' 💬
Regina Toal

11 Friday

★ *This week's angel-inspired word is FUTURE*

12 Saturday

13 Sunday

♥ *Angel lesson*

You will be angel-led into a wonderful life if you're willing to follow.

APRIL 2014 *Week 16*

14 Monday

15 Tuesday ○

★ *This week's angel-inspired word is BEGINNINGS*

16 Wednesday

17 Thursday

'Once you find who you are... the journey is bliss.' 💬
Siobhan Delaney

18 Friday

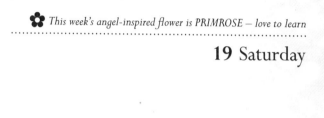 *This week's angel-inspired flower is PRIMROSE — love to learn*

19 Saturday

20 Sunday

 *Angel lesson*

It's never too late for a new start.

21 Monday

22 Tuesday ◑

This week's angel-inspired flower is BROOM — show humility ✿

23 Wednesday

'Peace forms your feathers and love shapes your wings… fly.'
Lyn-Marie Crane

24 Thursday

25 Friday

★ *This week's angel-inspired word is UNDERSTANDING*

26 Saturday

27 Sunday

♥ *Angel lesson*
You have to become a willing pupil to allow your angels teach you.

28 Monday

This week's angel-inspired flower is OLEANDER — don't jump in without thinking ✿

29 Tuesday ●

This week's angel-inspired word is SAFETY ★

30 Wednesday

Pagan Festival of Beltane: the day that commemorates the Union between God and Goddess.

1 Thursday

May

When you see all the cruelty in the world, it's tempting to just shut down and retreat into your own little world. But everyone does things for a reason. Those reasons might be misguided or have been instilled by indoctrination, creating monsters out of human beings. Yet if you can just step back for a moment from your gut reaction, you might find that you can have merciful thoughts towards people who seem violent and unattractive. Question why they are like that rather than reacting by simply condemning them. After all, you won't be able to heal the whole world unless you try to change their world first.

WHAT SHOULD YOU FOCUS ON?

This is the month to nurture your ability to show mercy. May is always a very powerful month for overcoming personal challenges and is therefore a great time for you to try to make a difference to the people of the world. Forgiveness and tolerance are a good starting point, but you must also project your light. If you imagine the world as a gigantic lantern of hope but dimmed by the smoke and writhing shadows of people in fear and despair, then see your own energy as bright and golden so that you can make a difference by adding it to the lantern. If everyone did this, the lantern would soon be too bright to look at and its brilliance really could change the whole world.

PLANET OF THE MONTH – VENUS

Venus is the symbol of unity and reminds you that we're all connected. No man is an island. Some of the people you think of as tyrants may even be people you wronged in a past life, and they may be acting out their fear or anger from that lifetime. By exploring such possibilities and accepting them, you will be brightening your own 'light'. The more lights that burn brightly, the greater the chances are that everyone's light will soon become brighter. So the way you see things does have a cumulative effect on everyone and everything in the universe.

KAHSHANNA'S STORY

This happened on a day that dimmed the light of the worlds for many, but still her angels found a way to give her hope.

My angelic experience took about seven years to process after what I saw on September 11, 2001. I watched from inside Chelsea Piers as the second World Trade Center tower crumbled and then I hitchhiked up to Harlem. Some very generous Dominican people were kind enough to offer me a lift and anyone else who would fit in the small, chugging vehicle. I still feel deeply compassionate at their gesture of not wanting any money. They just wished to help and understood that everyone needed to get home.

In the years that followed I researched healing and wellness, much of which entailed retreats to cultivate and experience some of the traditions and healing techniques I'd later offer to clients. In that time I was able to name and access my own intuitive and healing gifts and remove energy blocks. Receiving a healing session or an illumination session as it is called, seven years after 9/11, I lay down, fully clothed, and began the breathing portion of the session, which a seasoned wellness practitioner was offering me. I had been feeling off; small things were upsetting me but my deeper emotions seemed out of reach, despite all of the work I had done on wellness, Reiki, yoga and meditation... this one I could not do alone. So I asked for help.

I found myself taken back to 9/11... I was witnessing it again but there was a difference. I heard a voice direct me, in this waking dream state, and the next image I saw was a beautiful, radiant and softly glowing light. The people who had died didn't know what had happened and were walking into that light, greeted by angels. It was incredible. I saw people I'd never met looking confused and then being looked after by the angels I had only read about in school books.

ANGIE'S STORY

This story shows that angels and compassion do work together.

Once I was getting into my car in the dark and an urgent voice told me, "Quick, lock your door!" So I did. Almost immediately a man approached my car and tried the door handle. He was angry the door was locked, and he shouted a lot of abuse before putting his head into his hands and crouching on the ground. We locked eyes and

I remember willing this man to seek help. As I drove off he put his hand up in a friendly way and I took that to mean he had understood. I felt this was meant to happen to show this man that people do have compassion and also to give him the courage to seek help.

NOREEN'S STORY

I was really worried as I had to ask my boss for a raise, because otherwise I was going to lose my rented flat. I'd never been one to blow my own trumpet or stand my ground in the past but I was determined that this time would be different.

On the way to work I saw a shield drawn with chalk on the pavement, so I stopped to have a good look at it. It was very impressive and I had to admire it. The drawing had a big impact on me, but I didn't really know why. It was very colourful and had a kind of 3-D effect, and I did wonder who could have been skilful enough to do it and why. The shield was quite ornate and yet I couldn't really make sense of the drawings depicted on it. Were they some kind of birds?

When I met with my boss later that morning, I had the image of the shield still in my mind. He started talking as if to pre-empt what I was going to ask – I felt he already knew what it was, and was going to say no without even hearing me out – so I just started talking, too. For once I was articulate and strong and able to point out all the extras I'd done and how he'd be in trouble without me. Bizarrely my boss put up no fight at all and I got my raise easier than I'd ever dreamed possible.

On my way out the door that night I was looking forward to seeing the shield again, to have a better look at it, as I really felt it had helped me somehow. But when I reached the place where it had been, it was completely gone. It hadn't rained all day and yet there wasn't even a smear of chalk left. It was as if it had been absorbed into me or had been there especially for me to see.

ANGELS IN THE NEWS

In Israel some motorists filmed a strange fiery light that seems to be travelling along the central reservation. Is it an angel or something else? You can view the film by using the link in Resources section at the end of the diary.

ANGEL SYMBOL FOR MAY

Seeing a shield in an unusual place can be a sign from your guardian angel that you have some sort of confrontation coming, but your angel will give you the right words to say.

APRIL/MAY 2014 *Week 18*

28 Monday

This week's angel-inspired flower is OLEANDER – don't jump in without thinking 🌸

29 Tuesday ●

This week's angel-inspired word is SAFETY ⭐

30 Wednesday

Pagan Festival of Beltane: the day that commemorates the Union between God and Goddess.

1 Thursday

2 Friday

3 Saturday

'Angels make me feel guided, happy and safe!' Rada Kosanović

4 Sunday

♥ *Angel lesson*

There is no place safer for your soul than in an angel's shadow.

MAY 2014 *Week 19*

5 Monday

This week's angel-inspired flower is RAGGED ROBIN — healing will come to you ❀

6 Tuesday

7 Wednesday ◑

'The angels' love helps me to hold on.' Tennessee Jackson 🗨

8 Thursday

9 Friday

10 Saturday

★ *This week's angel-inspired word is IMAGINE*

11 Sunday

 *Angel lesson*

Don't let doubt cloud your visions.

MAY 2014 *Week 20*

12 Monday

....

13 Tuesday

'My angel always takes the reins to show me which way to go.'
Chaz Thompson
....

14 Wednesday ○

....

15 Thursday

This week's angel-inspired flower is HEATHER – listen to
your heart ✿
....

16 Friday

★ *This week's angel-inspired word is SOAR*

17 Saturday

18 Sunday

 *Angel lesson*

*Let your angel lift you to the stratosphere
and glimpse the wonder of you.*

MAY 2014 *Week 21*

19 Monday

'Morning, noon and night, our angels shine their light.'
Michelle Willman

20 Tuesday

21 Wednesday ◑

22 Thursday

This week's angel-inspired word is DEPEND ★

23 Friday

24 Saturday

❀ *This week's angel-inspired flower is PANSY*
– think before you speak or act

25 Sunday

♥ *Angel lesson*

Angels are always waiting to help you, but you must ask.

MAY 2014 *Week 22*

26 Monday

27 Tuesday

This week's angel-inspired word is ALLEGIANCE ★

28 Wednesday ●

This weeks angel-inspired flower is HYDRANGEA — keep talking and avoid misunderstandings ✿

29 Thursday

30 Friday

🗨 *'Angels guide you to where you need to be.' Michael Hunter*

31 Saturday

1 Sunday

🤍 *Angel lesson*

Don't be afraid to stand up and tell the world you believe in angels.

June

This month things can change very quickly and the balance between desirable and undesirable events is very tricky, so be careful what you wish for and how you wish for it. This is the month to make your cosmic shopping list. Think it through and always write things as if you already have them – so 'I am happy', rather than 'I will be happy', because as the universe sends you events to match your emotions, if you're 'wanting' something then you will always remain 'wanting' it. Write your list with a heart that already feels the joy of the events you're asking for, and then more joyous events will be reflected back to you.

WHAT SHOULD YOU FOCUS ON?

Things you've always dreamed of can start to come to pass at this time, but you still have to have patience. Just as Mother Nature's children, the plants, are blooming but not yet fruiting, this is a time to watch your plans start to fall into place. The main harvest, as with the Earth, will come later. Trust and acceptance are important now. As events around you unfold, have faith that your universal map will be clear very soon. You can also start to change anything you feel is stale about your life this month, as everything is open to change, including your appearance, where you live, your job, your relationships, and so on.

PLANET OF THE MONTH – MERCURY

The word, 'mercurial' comes from the name of this planet, and means things are fluid and can change direction if the flow is blocked or diverted in any way. Mercury is also known as Hermes, the winged messenger of the gods, so it's no surprise that during this month any kind of spiritual communication will be strong, whether you're trying to contact a loved one who has passed away or send your wishes for the future to the universe. The only possible drawback will be if you allow your intellect to override your intuition. So let your creative side have free rein, and don't allow your head to stop you from communicating spiritually.

JESSIE'S STORY

This shows how magical connections can be made at this time.

I loved my sister in-law very much. Out of my whole family, including those of my blood, she was the one who really understood me and gave me her support. When she died a couple of years ago, I was very sad. About two weeks after she had passed over I was sitting on my bed feeling very down and crying, when something made me look up — and there she was sitting on the end of the sofa as if it were perfectly normal for her to be there. Despite my amazement, I managed to notice that although she'd died of a wasting disease and had weighed very little at the end, she now appeared looking very beautiful and how she'd been before she got ill. I was still astounded to see her there so I asked her, "How can you be here?"

She replied, "You didn't think I wouldn't be back to keep an eye on you, did you?" She smiled, and then started to fade away — her smile was the last part of her to vanish, just like the Cheshire Cat! I felt so much better than I had for ages, and although I'd always thought that seeing a spirit would make me scared, it just wasn't like that at all. It was as if she'd popped in to say hello, just like she used to, and she wasn't really dead. It was wonderful.

MEL'S STORY

How an angel brought communication from someone who had passed away without their loved ones knowing.

A few years ago, my brother-in-law got word that his brother had been missing for several days. Of course, my brother-in-law and his family were very upset. I went over to visit him and keep him company for a while. Just half a mile into the drive home I saw a figure standing in the middle of the street. It was a tall, transparent male figure. He pointed firmly in the direction of my brother-in-law's home. I was shocked because it happened so very quickly. I braked instinctively but it was too late, and I drove my car through him. I looked anxiously in my rear-view mirror because I thought I'd hit the figure and he would be lying down in the street, but there was no-one there.

As startled as I was, I somehow knew that seeing the figure meant that my brother-in-law's brother had died, and sure enough he had. When I shared the story of the figure with my brother-in-law and his wife, they were equally stunned. Until this day, I'm utterly amazed how angels can appear out of nowhere and deliver messages very quickly when a loved one has passed away.

ANGELS IN THE NEWS

In London there's a building known as Topper's House. And one New Year's Eve four people decided to kill themselves by jumping from the roof of the building. Among them were the daughter of the Junior Minister of Education and a TV presenter called Martin Sharp. Believing themselves ready to die, they were just about to jump off the roof when all four heard a voice behind them, and they turned around to see who could be there with them. They described a man who reminded one of them of the film star, Matt Damon. However this being was floating above the ground, and his figure was misty and insubstantial. The four people were all filled with such a sense of joy in the being's presence that they no longer felt like ending their lives, but instead wanted overwhelmingly to live and share their joy with other people.

ANGEL SYMBOL FOR JUNE

At this time of year, after heavy rain and dark clouds, you may sometimes see the skies around you warmed by a magical golden glow, which lights up the tree-tops in a mystical-looking way. This is a message sent by your angels to keep alive your wonder in the world.

30 Friday

'Angels guide you to where you need to be.' Michael Hunter

31 Saturday

1 Sunday

♥ *Angel lesson*

Don't be afraid to stand up and tell the world you believe in angels.

JUNE 2014 *Week 23*

....

2 Monday

This week's angel-inspired flower is DAFFODIL — be extra polite and chivalrous ❁
....

3 Tuesday

....

4 Wednesday

'Every step in the darkness is a step towards the light.' 💬
Alison Andrews
....

5 Thursday ☽

....

6 Friday

....

7 Saturday

★ *This week's angel-inspired word is DECENCY*
....

8 Sunday

....

 *Angel lesson*
Keep your integrity at all times.

JUNE 2014 *Week 24*

9 Monday

10 Tuesday

This week's angel-inspired word is ACHIEVE ★

11 Wednesday

12 Thursday

This week's angel-inspired flower is BEGONIA — use your imagination ✿

○ **13** Friday

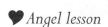 *'Angels inspire you when you least expect it.'* Christina Christou

14 Saturday

15 Sunday

♥ *Angel lesson*

*Once you understand your goal, take baby steps
towards it and your angel will help you.*

JUNE 2014 *Week 25*

16 Monday

17 Tuesday

This week's angel-inspired word is BOUNDLESS ★

18 Wednesday

19 Thursday ◑

'Belief in your angels is belief in yourself.' Lynn Kilpatrick 🗩

20 Friday

 *This week's angel-inspired flower is IRIS — expect good news*

21 Saturday

Pagan festival of Litha: this festival is the opposite to Yule, being the longest day of the year. It's when the very first crops are gathered. In times gone by, people would work together all day to bring in the early harvest.

22 Sunday

♥ *Angel lesson*

Your body may be finite, but your soul is infinite.

23 Monday

'Put faith in your angels: trust they'll show you the way.'
Regina Toal

24 Tuesday

25 Wednesday

This week's angel-inspired flower is ORCHID — look for the smallest beauty ❀

26 Thursday

● **27** Friday

28 Saturday

★ *This week's angel-inspired word is STRIVE*

29 Sunday

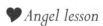 *Angel lesson*

Angels love people who try, so never give up.

JUNE/JULY 2014 *Week 27*

30 Monday

1 Tuesday

This week's angel-inspired flower is AGRIMONY — be grateful

2 Wednesday

3 Thursday

'Angel maths: count your blessings, add thanks — watch them multiply.'
Silverla St.Michael

July

This is the time when you find the summer moving too fast
and you can start to feel overtaken by events. You're half
way through, but half way through to where? You need to
stop and take stock. Are you still following the river of your
dreams, or have you floated off blissfully unaware down a
smaller stream? It can be difficult to stay on course and
shoot the rapids with their turbulent yet exhilarating white
water, when drifting peacefully and effortlessly down a
smoother watercourse seems so very tempting. Pull yourself
back and reassess your dreams. Don't give up at this point.
A lot of time has already passed this year, but there's plenty
ahead of you still and your power is growing.

WHAT SHOULD YOU FOCUS ON?

This month you need to plot a straight course to where you want and know you need to go. Try not to get distracted by temporary pleasures, or at least not at the expense of your true path. And don't settle for less than you really need. Sometimes in life it's easier just to say, 'This will do,' when in your heart of hearts you know that you'll be disappointed further down the line if you settle for mediocrity.

Happiness in this life will only come from fulfilling what you set out to do before you were born. We can fill our lives with trivia and make ourselves believe that the next sought-after possession will be the one that brings us real happiness at last, but it's all smoke and mirrors. These things will bring a temporary burst of joy, but it will be short lived, and our perception that others admire us for what we own will be even more fleeting. In the long term this is like a sugary snack that only sustains you for a tiny while, leaving you to 'come down' from the sugar rush into a dissatisfied state. You were provided with a true path to happiness for this life – it was programmed into you before you came here, and following this is the only way to find enduring contentment. If you need a reminder of your true purpose, make sure to meditate and ask your angels to help you to recall your mission. Just as when you usually call on your angels to help you, make sure you clearly state your intent as to what the communication should be about before you start.

PLANET OF THE MONTH – SATURN

Saturn is the planet of fire and it represents your own inner fire. It is also the symbol for 'coming of age'. We are all influenced by our parents and their patterns of behaviour and beliefs, to a greater or lesser extent. Of course, this influence is important and should not be abandoned. However, we all have our own path to walk, and this is the time to start to have faith in that. Believe that you have your own power inside you and you can move mountains. Don't lose faith in yourself in this mid-month of the year. Don't use your power to argue or battle over trivial things, respect your inner power and call on it wisely. When you call on your angels, use that inner voice that comes from your centre, as if you're summoning, rather than asking, and you'll be amazed at what can happen. Concentrating on this planet and using it as a focus for meditation will enable you to build in an automatic alert system in your subconscious, so that events in your life that need long term vigilance, such as constantly checking to see if you're following your right path and haven't been distracted, won't ever get overlooked.

CONCETTA'S STORY

From an early age I was visited by an angel who told me I'd never have children of my own. As I grew up I wanted the things that most young girls want — to get married and have a family. But I always remembered what the angel had told me. It wasn't until I met and married my husband John that I really started to worry about her message.

I'd only been married a short time when I had a tubular pregnancy that involved surgery. I was devastated. But again I was visited by angels, this time telling me everything would be all right. I was told that I had a special mission for this life, which I didn't understand at the time.

As the first couple years of my marriage passed by, I became confused. When I'd been younger, the same angels who told me I wouldn't have children had also told me that I'd have something to do with raising children. Yet when I married John, who has two children from his first marriage, it truly didn't dawn on me that these were the children I was to be involved with raising. And the angels were still visiting me, trying to help me let go of my goal to have children of my own. That was very, very hard for me to do. I couldn't fathom what else could possibly fill my life.

I was also having difficulty with my husband's family, who never had taken to me. Knowing that they would all be happy if I couldn't have children made this experience all the more painful. I just couldn't give up. Now I invested in in-vitro treatment, my last resort. But, nothing.

And still angels were present in my life, continuing to reassure me that there was something I would be able to contribute, something I'd be able to give to life, to others' lives. You might think that with all this heavenly reassurance I would be at peace. But I had no notion of the role I was to play in life. To say that I was angry and disillusioned with life would be to put it mildly. I was so unhappy. I felt betrayed by God. I felt useless as a woman.

Slowly — very slowly — I made a choice to believe what the angels were telling me. I made a choice to trust God. And slowly I began to see the light. I began my work with the Other Side; I started to realize the importance of the work I was doing, that this was my contribution. That, even without having children I do make a difference to many in this life here on Earth. I have a stepdaughter who is also "my" daughter. She loves me and is one of my best friends. I have grandchildren; I receive Mother's Day cards. What the angels told me is true: without having children of my own, I'm still a mother.

ANGELS IN THE NEWS

Following a car crash on Highway 6 in Texas, Lisa and Anthony were trapped in their respective cars. Both cars caught fire and both drivers were certain they were going to die. Anthony passed out from the smoke. A couple called Cheri and Cody stopped to help but couldn't pull Lisa from her car because it was too crushed. They cried to the angels for help, and all three of them saw a pair of hands of light reach through the wreckage and grab Cody's hands where they clasped Lisa's, and suddenly they were both outside the car. In the meantime, another passer-by could see Anthony slumped in his car as it exploded. She prayed and Anthony suddenly floated free of the car.

ANGEL SYMBOL FOR JULY

Rainbows are natural phenomena, but if you've asked for an answer or a sign and a rainbow immediately appears, accept it, because angels are a force of nature and can easily use natural events to contact you.

30 Monday

1 Tuesday

This week's angel-inspired flower is AGRIMONY – be grateful ✿

2 Wednesday

3 Thursday

'Angel maths: count your blessings, add thanks – watch them multiply.'
Silverla StMichael

4 Friday

★ *This week's angel-inspired word is GRATITUDE*

◐ **5** Saturday

6 Sunday

♥ *Angel lesson*

*Be thankful for every little thing your angel
brings you, no matter how small.*

JULY 2014 *Week 28*

7 Monday

This week's angel-inspired flower is AMARYLLIS — enhance your self-esteem ✿

8 Tuesday

9 Wednesday

This week's angel-inspired word is ENCOURAGEMENT ★

10 Thursday

11 Friday

○ **12** Saturday

💬 *'A baby's smile, a helpful hand, a generous gesture... all angels.'*
Christina Christou

13 Sunday

💙 *Angel lesson*
If you're feeling down, tell your angel and ask for some kindness.

JULY 2014 *Week 29*

14 Monday

'Angels wipe your tears away with their heavenly touch.'
Lynn Kilpatrick

15 Tuesday

This week's angel-inspired word is DEFENDED ★

16 Wednesday

17 Thursday

18 Friday

◑ **19** Saturday

✿ *This week's angel-inspired flower is FERN — feel protected*

20 Sunday

♥ *Angel lesson*
Love, and especially the love of angels, really can conquer all.

JULY 2014 *Week 30*

21 Monday

This week's angel-inspired flower is ANEMONE — anticipate love ❁

22 Tuesday

23 Wednesday

'Let kindness be your heart that beats for others' souls.'
Lesley Jane Hazelhurst

24 Thursday

25 Friday

★ *This week's angel-inspired word is ENVISAGE*

● **26** Saturday

27 Sunday

♥ *Angel lesson*
Only see what you want to have happen, not what you do not.

JULY 2014 *Week 31*

....

28 Monday

This week's angel-inspired word is LAUGH ★
....

29 Tuesday

....

30 Wednesday

This week's angel-inspired flower is DELPHINIUM –
be joyful and have fun ✿
....

31 Thursday

....

August

It's magical mid-summer, when anything can happen.
Journalists call this the 'silly season' when strange things
occur, and you can make use of the energy that's available
at this unusual time. This is when you should be able to
come into your full power. You should be realizing your
dreams for the year and your dreams for humanity. It's a
time to congratulate yourself on what you have achieved
and create a real sense of belief that you can achieve a lot
more yet. It's a good idea at this point to take a break if you
can, to escape from mundane matters and indulge yourself.

WHAT SHOULD YOU FOCUS ON?

Focus on the people in your life who continue to be domineering. Try and understand that they are only that way because they're insecure. You have a chance now while you're at your highest psychic power to help them transform into people with a benevolent purpose. If you succeed in this you will take another huge step towards being able to channel even higher. This is the time to focus on a challenge of this sort that you might not have had to confidence to do before.

PLANET OF THE MONTH – CHIRON

The name of this planet comes from a centaur: the half-man, half-horse creature of Greek mythology. This planet is an escapee from the outer Solar System that should have held it captive, but did not succeed. You, too, should use the properties of this planet to help you escape – from danger, but also from materialism. Dive boldly into your spiritual knowledge and your inner self at this time. Throw out logic and believe.

JONNO'S STORY

One night about two years ago, I was feeling so low that I decided to kill myself. There didn't seem to be anyone who needed or cared about me and I felt so alone. My parents had recently died and my wife had left me, taking our children with her. My house was mortgaged up to the hilt and I was likely to lose it. I hated my job and it didn't pay well. It was no wonder then that I felt I had nothing to live for.

I didn't want to involve anyone else in my suicide so I was going to drive my car into a bridge, before it could be repossessed. I set off to do just that, but on the way there something magical happened. I'm a fellow who drank a lot and I was, I confess, also a bit macho. I didn't have a spiritual bone in my body, but when I saw a light glowing at the side of the road, I simply had to pull over and investigate. It was just hovering there with no apparent source that I could see. It was blue and reflected off the sandy ground at the side of the road. It was really eerie. I got out and walked over to the light. I still couldn't see any reason for it, and it crossed my mind that maybe it was my easy way out. Maybe if I walked into it, I'd just get absorbed, really quickly. So, taking a deep breath I walked right into the light and then, as if someone flicked a switch, it went out. It was pretty dark and also preternaturally quiet, and everything felt muffled. There was not a sound: no traffic noise from the distant freeway, nothing.

WHAT SHOULD YOU FOCUS ON?

Then I heard it — a pathetic, whimpering noise. I still couldn't see much, only from the side-wash of my headlights, so I felt along the ground that was almost hot to touch and came across something fluffy. It was a hairy little body. As I picked it up something warm and wet licked my hands. I took it back to the light, which revealed a scruffy little dog, It had obviously been hit, was covered in blood, scared and in pain, but it didn't bite.

To cut a long story short, once I took this little thing to the vet I then took responsibility for him, and he turned into my best pal. I couldn't think of leaving him. The weird thing was, I chose that road for its remoteness and I can't understand how this little dog got out there, or how he was struck by a car, because I never saw another vehicle in the ten miles I drove first one way and then the other, up and down it.

Things are slowly getting better for me and my little pal.

ANGELS IN THE NEWS

A man called Bruce Van Natta was virtually cut in half by a massive logging truck he was working on, when the jack holding it up gave way. His waist area was crushed to a depth of one inch by the 12,000lbs that fell on him. He was in terrible pain. His back was broken and five major blood vessels were severed as well as his intestines being totally crushed. His colleague pulled him out a little way at Bruce's insistence.

When Bruce then prayed for help, the pain vanished completely. He floated up out of his body and looked down from the ceiling where he could see his work colleague kneeling beside his shattered body. On either side of the body there were two glowing figures holding his body together. He believes they were angels and he was given the choice to return to his body or to leave. He chose to stay and despite not being expected to live, he recovered – even his intestines grew back, which is unheard of. Bruce Van Natta's story can be read in his book, 'Saved By Angels'.

ANGEL SYMBOL FOR AUGUST
Animals are often used by angels as messengers, so if you come across one in an unexpected place, look up the symbolism of that particular animal to discover what its presence might mean to you.

1 Friday

Pagan Festival of Lughnasdh: also known as Lammas Eve and marks the first harvest of the year.

2 Saturday

🗨 *'God's angels catch us so we won't fall!' Simon Oliver*

3 Sunday

💜 *Angel lesson*

Laughter is good medicine and angels do have a sense of humour.

AUGUST 2014 *Week 32*

4 Monday ☽

This week's angel-inspired flower is POTENTILLA — indulge in some
pampering and learn to love yourself ❁

5 Tuesday

6 Wednesday

'Listen to your heart. It's your angel speaking to you.' 🗩
Sarah Ann Kerr

7 Thursday

8 Friday

9 Saturday

★ *This week's angel-inspired word is NURTURE*

○ **10** Sunday

♥ *Angel lesson*
Even if you're alone in the world, your angel will always tend you.

11 Monday

....

12 Tuesday

This week's angel-inspired word is DETERMINATION ★
....

13 Wednesday

This week's angel-inspired flower is VALERIAN — think of all the good times ✿
....

14 Thursday

....

15 Friday

'Shine your angelic light for all to be guided by.' Simon Oliver

16 Saturday

17 Sunday

♥ *Angel lesson*
Stay focused and you can accomplish anything.

AUGUST 2014 *Week 34*

18 Monday

This week's angel-inspired flower is GARDENIA — expect secret love to be revealed

19 Tuesday

20 Wednesday

21 Thursday

'Each and all of us are truly unique and more powerful than we know.'
Regina Toal

22 Friday

23 Saturday

★ *This week's angel-inspired word is HOPEFULNESS*

24 Sunday

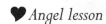 *Angel lesson*

Positive energy can move mountains.

AUGUST 2014 *Week 35*

25 Monday ●

26 Tuesday

This week's angel-inspired word is WISDOM ★

27 Wednesday

28 Thursday

This week's angel-inspired flower is ROSE — be happy with what you've achieved ✿

29 Friday

🗨 *'Angels light my world.' Mary J O'Donohoe*

30 Saturday

31 Sunday

💜 *Angel lesson*

Never forget, you are here to learn.

September

At this time we start to reap many harvests: the harvest of food, the harvest of friendship gained through the year, the harvest of our endeavours. It's a very rich month in nature, full of fruit just starting to appear. It can make us feel lazy, as if perhaps all our work is done and we can rest on our laurels. But, the harvest won't be safely gathered until October, and everything could still come to nothing. Keep manifesting your new reality, which you've been working on all year until now. The more you can see it, the more you can make it happen. If doubts or complacency start to creep in, then the effect will be similar to cancelling an order, so remain committed.

WHAT SHOULD YOU FOCUS ON?

This month focus on strengthening the connection to your angels, because you still need them very much. I'm sure there will have been times during reading this diary that you've thought, *If only I could have that connection and do what's being asked!* So, the first step towards strengthening your angel connection is to *believe* in it. Believe you are worthy of your angel's love no matter what; believe that your angel does want to help you; believe that you can establish a deep connection. It's quite a difficult concept for we humans to accept – because there are very few, if any, people we know who give us unconditional love in this world, but our angels are linked to us in a way that can never be broken. Even people we perceive to be 'evil' are loved by their angels, no matter what they do. Knowing this, it's not that hard to accept that those of us who are just 'normal' are also loved eternally by our angels. So, next time you start a meditation, try beginning by feeling for that love. It's easier than you think. Once you do feel, the rest will be easy.

September is also a good time to reflect on whether or not there are people in your life you've shown too much hostility towards, or areas in it that you've been too complacent with. Make sure that your energy and your power are balanced, so that by the end of the year, or even by next month, everything you've worked for will come to fruition – beautifully ripe, and ready for picking.

PLANET OF THE MONTH – URANUS

Uranus is the symbol of unpredictability and can help you survive any twists and unexpected turns that might threaten all you strive for. It can also aid you in achieving the necessary balances in your life. Because of its reputation for the unexpected, Uranus can bring miracles. Uranus is known as the planet of procreation, so if you long for a child this would be a good time to try to conceive, especially if you've come to think that this is one miracle you will never achieve. Any child conceived at this time will be very much an individual – a special child – and he or she will grow up to become a person of influence in the world. This child might not be easy to raise, as they will have a strong will and a need to express their own creativity. This could manifest in anything from decorating the wallpaper with their infant artwork to not being able to wait to produce their own offspring. But the difficulties will be worth it as you will have the satisfaction of knowing you played a part in creating this person.

SCOTT'S STORY

This tells of a disaster averted by angels.

We were on a trip in a rental car in the middle of nowhere. It was snowing and we were on an isolated stretch of the Glenwood Canyon in Colorado late in the evening. Suddenly some rocks fell down the mountainside and blocked our path, sending our car into a ditch. We also had a flat tyre from the impact. I had a terrible sinking feeling as not only did we have to get the car out of the ditch, but the trunk was full, which would make it difficult to get out the tools and the spare tyre. The highway emergency phone wasn't working so we couldn't send for help.

It was getting darker and it was really unlikely that anyone would come by, but I didn't panic because I always send angels ahead when I travel. So I wasn't totally surprised when out of nowhere several young people suddenly appeared. Within minutes the trunk was unpacked, the tyre was changed and they'd called the rental company on a mobile phone to arrange a replacement car at the next town, as our car now sported a temporary tyre.

It all happened so fast and was too 'convenient'. Not only that but the young people who had saved us just disappeared into the night as mysteriously as they had come.

JACQUI'S STORY

This gives another example of how angels will help when they know we're ready to listen.

One winter, my first as a driver, I had my first trip out in snow. I skidded badly and had no idea what to do. I'd been told of course, but at that moment I just couldn't remember. The car slid from one bank to the other and I thought it would tip right over. I pleaded for somebody to help me. Suddenly I heard a voice speaking as clear as a bell. It said, "Steer into the skid". As soon as I did so, the car came back under control. Obviously I wasn't alone in the car! I'm certain my guardian angel heard my thoughts and said just what I needed to hear.

EVE'S STORY

I was on my way home from the funeral of a dear friend, the brother of my best friend, who herself had only passed away three weeks before. You can imagine how upset I was – it was heartbreaking. I was invited back to the family's house but just could not face all that again.

I know I should have walked around the gardens to get my head straight before riding my moped home, but I just wanted to go, so I headed off. Tears were streaming down my face – my best friend was gone, and now her brother. I felt so low.

As I indicated to pull out from the slip road onto the main road, a car behind me flashed to let me out. He was indicating to take the flyover to the left of me. As he passed me he looked at me and gave me the thumbs-up sign. At that moment the love he sent hit me in the chest like a bullet. I was so overwhelmed with love I just had to smile and once again thank my angels.

ANGELS IN THE NEWS

In New York State, a woman called Rose found herself trapped in her car. She'd hit the barrier at the side of the freeway, her airbag had inflated and she was dazed. When she found herself safely outside the car and looked back, she couldn't believe she'd escaped injury-free. But then she saw a photo of her car taken by Sharon, a photographer from the fire department. In the photo a white, winged, classic angel-shape made of mist can be seen standing in front of the car. This shape even appears in the negative of the photo, so it's hard to believe that it could be a fake.

ANGEL SYMBOL FOR SEPTEMBER

This month's symbol is feathers. When you're hoping for this sign from your angels, you need to look for the unusual – for example brightly coloured feathers or feathers in unlikely places, such as inside.

SEPTEMBER 2014 *Week 36*

. . . .

1 Monday

This week's angel-inspired flower is GLADIOLUS — stand in your own truth ❁

. . . .

2 Tuesday ◗

. . . .

3 Wednesday

'Amplify your light — it creates bridges upon which angels tread.'
Silverla StMichael

. . . .

4 Thursday

. . . .

5 Friday

6 Saturday

 *This week's angel-inspired word is BRAVERY*

7 Sunday

♥ *Angel lesson*
Have courage, for you are immortal.

SEPTEMBER 2014 *Week 37*

8 Monday

9 Tuesday ○

This week's angel-inspired word is EVALUATE ★

10 Wednesday

11 Thursday

This week's angel-inspired flower is ORANGE BLOSSOM – expect news of a pregnancy ✿

12 Friday

'Angels are love in its purest form.' Liz Ferguson

13 Saturday

14 Sunday

♥ *Angel lesson*
Take stock every day and see what you have to be grateful for.

SEPTEMBER 2014 *Week 38*

. . . .

15 Monday

This week's angel-inspired flower is SEA PINK – all will be harmonious ✿

. . . .

16 Tuesday ☾

. . . .

17 Wednesday

'Golden light shines down from angels on smiles of happiness.'
Lynn Kilpatrick

. . . .

18 Thursday

. . . .

19 Friday

20 Saturday

⭐ *This week's angel-inspired word is CONCORD*

21 Sunday

♥ *Angel lesson*

Try and be conciliatory whenever possible.

SEPTEMBER 2014 *Week 39*

22 Monday

This week's angel-inspired flower is THRIFT — allow your inner artist to come out

23 Tuesday

Pagan festival of Mabon: also known as the Autumn Equinox and the time of the main harvest. This is a time to begin to store supplies for the coming winter, so lots of pickling and freezing takes place.

24 Wednesday ●

25 Thursday

This week's angel-inspired word is ASSIST ★

26 Friday

🗨 *'Each time you give a kindness, you are working with your angels.'*
Michelle Willman

27 Saturday

28 Sunday

♥ *Angel lesson*

Help others as you would like your angel to help you.

SEPT/OCT 2014 *Week 40*

....

29 Monday

This week's angel-inspired word is DELIGHT ★
....

30 Tuesday

....

1 Wednesday ◗

This week's angel-inspired flower is NASTURTIUM — do something for others ✿
....

2 Thursday

....

October

Sometimes we start to feel a little vulnerable in this month, as Christmas seems to be looming, the weather often starts to get colder and winter is just around the corner. Because of this it's also easy to start doubting our spiritual connections. As a collective 'people' we have abused the planet we live upon, and so what we need to do at this time of year is deepen our connection to Mother Earth and give her our love and support. This will automatically deepen our connection to the universe. Similarly, we need to nurture, respect and love our other home — our physical body — because it, too, becomes vulnerable at this time of year.

WHAT SHOULD YOU FOCUS ON?

Think about the fact that your cells are created from the food you eat and give a lot of consideration to what you should be fuelling yourself with. If you've been guilty of rushing meals, using ready-cooked dinners to save time and effort, eating 'on the hoof', and putting things off until tomorrow, now is the time make some improvements. If you don't know how to cook, take some lessons. Stop smoking and drinking alcohol and give your body a chance to heal itself.

Once you've taken care of the inside of your body, start thinking about the outside – the environment your body lives in. Consider whether or not you're doing enough to recycle, to lessen the burden of your daily life upon the planet. Start buying appliances that have a smaller carbon footprint; try having things repaired rather than being one of the 'throw-away' society. Build on the love and respect you already have for the other creatures that share your home planet, and seriously consider becoming vegetarian, or even vegan. If this is not for you, at least take as many steps as you can towards helping to obliterate the daily cruelty that is visited upon some of our animal companions on this planet.

PLANET OF THE MONTH – EARTH

The Earth, apart from being vital to our survival, is also a symbol of unification. Everything on the planet travels through cycles – physical life and death being the obvious one. Water falls as rain, runs into rivers and out into the seas, rises again and falls as rain again. Crops seed, grow, mature and then die back to the soil. This is the natural way but over the centuries man has disrupted some of these processes. So, do your part in understanding that not only are we all connected with each other and so need to help and nurture each other, but we are also connected to the planet itself, to the rivers, to the trees, to the animals and the rocks.

Consider your actions at this time and acknowledge that even you, on your own, can make a difference. Think deeply about the miracle that created the Earth: the perfect synchronicity of conditions that allowed life to thrive here; the way in which the position of the axis, the magnetic field and the influence of the moon all play their miraculous parts; and understand that we must be very important to have caused such amazing cosmic engineering.

Earth is, of course, synonymous with another very emotive word – home. So as well as looking at the big picture this month, also consider how you can make the place you live in more welcoming to angels and so, inevitably, more comforting for all the family. To do this, try and make an angel sanctuary or a special meditation space in a small corner of your house or apartment and fill the place with warm 'earthy' colours, such as orange, yellow and terracotta. Or, if you have a garden, make an angel sanctuary or meditation space outside – this will also enable you to enhance your connection to the Earth we walk upon.

MARY'S STORY

This shows that angels can help you to take care of yourself and clear yourself from self-inflicted abuse, which can appear to be gratification and serve as a distraction from your true path.

I was an alcoholic, and one day I came to, after a blackout. When an alcoholic comes out of a black-out they're no longer drunk but quite sober, so they're quite frightened and ashamed, not knowing where they've been or who they have spent the last few hours with. Suddenly, with no preparation or expectation, I had a vision. It was like some curtains opened for a few minutes and I was able to peer beyond them to see what needed to be changed in my life.

There were enormous bright lights illuminating everything everywhere, a calm and warm atmosphere in which everything felt safe and angels were flying all about. I was bestowed with new knowledge about how I would have to change and I understood completely. It was as if the angels imparted this knowledge to me. There was an immense presence of love and healing in the air.

This scenario only lasted a few minutes because I understood and accepted the message right away, and then just basked in the love. After the moments of clarity had accomplished their purpose, the curtain closed. I went to bed, slept well, and upon rising, I started to follow the instructions. I have continued to lead my life according to the angels' advice and never looked back. I changed because of their visit and became a far better person.

ELIZABETH'S STORY

My dear late mother had cancer for over ten years. She was my best friend and a real inspiration because she bore her illness with such acceptance and fortitude. When she passed away, although I was overjoyed she was free from suffering, I was also very sad because she had always been there for us and to be truthful was a light in the family. A day or so after she passed over, I went to bed as usual. I'd not been sleeping too well, but that night I seemed to be overcome with weariness and I fell into a deep slumber. The strange thing was I also was awake because I felt enclosed by what I can only describe as warm, enfolding wings. I felt such peace and love as I'd never felt before and I knew it was an angel nursing me.

The next morning when I awoke I felt better than I had for ages and I knew that it was my angel who had brought me comfort, as well as the will to look after my father, who was also grieving. Although he had not acknowledged such experiences before, Dad believed my account and said it was an angel sent by my mother to help us.

ANGELS IN THE NEWS

After a terrible storm and tornado in Salem, Indiana, a little girl, appropriately called Angel, was found lying in a field surrounded by the bodies of her family. Angel mysteriously survived, while her whole family perished around her. She was found 40 miles from home and no one can explain how she survived, except to say that perhaps her name-sakes, the other 'angels', must have saved her.

ANGEL SYMBOL FOR OCTOBER

Sometimes in the autumn you'll experience an amazing morning if you get up early. As the sun rises on a fine day, there will be a pink, pearly mist everywhere. I always think the angels have sent it to remind me of the magic that is all around me which I sometimes don't see.

SEPT/OCT 2014 *Week 40*

29 Monday

This week's angel-inspired word is DELIGHT ★

30 Tuesday

1 Wednesday ☽

This week's angel-inspired flower is NASTURTIUM — do something for others ✿

2 Thursday

3 Friday

4 Saturday

'Live, love, be happy, for that is your role in life.' Christina Christou

5 Sunday

♥ *Angel lesson*
If you have something to be cheerful about, revel in it.

OCTOBER 2014 *Week 41*

6 Monday

....

7 Tuesday

'I see visions of angels in rainbows of light.' Ruthie Young 💬
....

8 Wednesday ○

This week's angel-inspired flower is HYACINTH — exercise and nurture your body ✿
....

9 Thursday

....

Week 41 OCTOBER 2014

10 Friday

⭐ *This week's angel-inspired word is ENTHUSIASM*

11 Saturday

12 Sunday

♥ *Angel lesson*
Encourage and feed your will to learn.

OCTOBER 2014 *Week 42*

13 Monday

This week's angel-inspired word is TENDERNESS

14 Tuesday

15 Wednesday

16 Thursday

'Listen to your inner voice, never doubt your first thought.'
Lyn-Marie Crane

17 Friday

18 Saturday

✿ *This week's angel-inspired flower is ELDERFLOWER*
— be gentle with others

19 Sunday

♥ *Angel lesson*

Show compassion towards yourself whenever you can.

OCTOBER 2014 *Week 43*

....

20 Monday

'Be an earth angel: practice peace, have hope, live love.'
Silverla StMichael

....

21 Tuesday

....

22 Wednesday

This week's angel-inspired flower is MAGNOLIA — appreciate the
natural world 🌼

....

23 Thursday ●

....

24 Friday

25 Saturday

★ *This week's angel-inspired word is EMPATHY*

26 Sunday

♥ *Angel lesson*
Make compassion your friend.

OCTOBER 2014 *Week 44*

27 Monday

28 Tuesday

This week's angel-inspired flower is VIOLET — be ready to grab an opportunity ✿

29 Wednesday

30 Thursday

This week's angel-inspired word is LIBERTY ★

● **31** Friday

*Pagan festival of Samhain: the end of harvest time.
It is also the time traditionally when the veil between those
living and those who have passed away is at its thinnest.*

1 Saturday

 *'Angels are only a breath away.'* Christina Christou

2 Sunday

💜 *Angel lesson*
Be free to believe in the spirit and you can open doors.

November

The year is rapidly drawing to a close, but there's still time before you get to the end to take stock and look back studiously over the year, to see if your priorities have changed at all. See if you need to change yourself or your life, as large or even minor adjustments now still take effect and can get you off to a much better start for 2015. This is also the time to appreciate and notice the 'teachers' who have come and perhaps gone from your life during the months that have passed. These teachers can have taken many forms, including loved ones, temporary acquaintances or work colleagues and they can also take the form of animals and children.

WHAT SHOULD YOU FOCUS ON?

This is the time to make sure you have noticed and understood whatever your teachers have tried to show you. At this point it should be possible for you to look back over the year behind you and see a map of sorts, showing you the true journey you've been on, which is often not quite what you might have thought. Sometimes you might have been a bit stubborn, and this is a natural reaction for most people as we don't like to be told what to do! But think – in doing so you might have refused your angel's help, so don't be embarrassed to admit you were wrong and ask for help. Angels always forgive.

PLANET OF THE MONTH – PLUTO

This planet can bring you explosive breakthroughs in your knowledge and understanding of your own spiritual journey. Pluto can show you the way ahead in projects that you had thought were dead in the water. You may have sudden insight into how to snatch success from defeat. This is the time when things can go either way as the scales are finely balanced. Let the lessons your teachers have shown you allow you to look deeply into yourself and your motives without fear of what you might find.

FREDA'S STORY

Tragedy scarred my mom's soul, and yet she clung to Jesus with childlike faith. The day that gnawed at her heart had happened two years before I was born when my brother died in a huge fire that burned their three-story house. Mom was able to get my sister out and break the fall of my aunt, who was seven months pregnant and had jumped from a second-storey window. The fire fighters had had to hold my mother back from going back into the flames to save her son.

Only a few years after the devastating tragedy, my sister was severely burned in an electric heater accident and was in the hospital for more than a month. My mother almost lost another child to fire. I think that God protected her by giving her that childlike faith.

My mom taught me so much. For instance, she taught me the immense value of friendship by her lifelong commitment to helping an elderly lady who was blind and almost deaf, and a family who had no car and needed help with shopping. Mother's life was truly remarkable and she blessed many people as she demonstrated selfless love.

Later a very rare complication of surgery occurred,

and Mom had a major stroke. Our world as young adults turned upside-down. Over the next few months, every tiny step of healing came as a miracle, borne of prayer and our deep love for her. She was in a coma for several months and then slowly she awakened and began to focus upon us. We appreciated the smallest moments of fun with her.

Her body was left partially paralyzed from the stroke, but God brought brightness to her life, as if she was still a five-year old child sitting on the Lord's lap. She was always happy, though she suffered much physically.

We were given several more years to enjoy my mother's company, to take in the love she had given us and return it to her. Then, all too soon, she became severely ill. Within just days, we knew Mom was dying. I stayed with her overnight at the hospital. I held her hand, prayed with her, sang to her and talked softly to her. I dozed and awoke to find her breathing was more laboured. Then her breathing became less frequent. I prayed again, releasing her to God's hands. When I opened my eyes, I sensed there were several angels in the room. I could not see them, but felt the presence of beings on a divine mission. When my dear mother's last breath was released and no other came, I felt her spirit was lifted from her body and escorted by these wondrous beings to God's Presence. Immediately, the temperature in the room fell by about 30 degrees. It was the frozen breath of death.

I had to leave. I scooped up my things, went to the nurses' station, reported that she had died and then broke down and wept. It was the most profound and beautiful thing, yet also the most difficult thing I have ever experienced.

ANGELS IN THE NEWS

A video taken by a road surveillance camera somewhere in China shows a man on a motorbike apparently missing certain death when a flash of unexplained light seems to snatch him from the path of a speeding truck. See the film using the link in Resources section and judge for yourself.

ANGEL SYMBOL FOR NOVEMBER

Butterflies are a well-known sign of angels. They often appear at the funerals of loved ones, especially in the cold months when they wouldn't normally be expected to be around.

◑ 31 Friday

Pagan festival of Samhain: the end of harvest time.
It is also the time traditionally when the veil between those
living and those who have passed away is at its thinnest.

1 Saturday

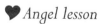 *'Angels are only a breath away.'* Christina Christou

2 Sunday

♥ *Angel lesson*
Be free to believe in the spirit and you can open doors.

NOVEMBER 2014 *Week 45*

....

3 Monday

This week's angel-inspired word is TOLERANCE ★
....

4 Tuesday

....

5 Wednesday

This week's angel-inspired flower is CARNATION — remember those in spirit ✿
....

6 Thursday ○

....

7 Friday

8 Saturday

'Angels lock their wings and carry us above the storm.'
Simon Oliver

9 Sunday

♥ *Angel lesson*
Don't judge others harshly.

NOVEMBER 2014 *Week 46*

10 Monday

11 Tuesday

'An angel's whisper cannot be heard over a noisy mind.'
Moira Fitzsimmons

12 Wednesday

13 Thursday

This week's angel-inspired flower is LOTUS — guard your thoughts and think only good ✿

◑ **14** Friday

★ *This week's angel-inspired word is DEVOTE*

15 Saturday

16 Sunday

♥ *Angel lesson*

You must make time for angels if you want them to spend time on you.

NOVEMBER 2014 *Week 47*

17 Monday

This week's angel-inspired word is RESPITE ★

18 Tuesday

19 Wednesday

'Don't look back — none of us is going that way.' Regina Toal

20 Thursday

21 Friday

● **22** Saturday

✿ *This week's angel-inspired flower is POPPY — expect sweet dreams*

23 Sunday

♥ *Angel lesson*
Relax sometimes; don't always be running.

NOVEMBER 2014 *Week 48*

24 Monday

25 Tuesday

'Angels love with their hearts, not with their eyes.'
Lyn-Marie Crane

26 Wednesday

27 Thursday

This week's angel-inspired flower is VALERIAN — think of all the good times in your life ❀

28 Friday

★ *This week's angel-inspired word is LOYALTY*

◑ **29** Saturday

30 Sunday

♥ *Angel lesson*

Angels are a constant in your life,
so make sure you are constantly in theirs.

December

So, we're finally at the end of another year, and I'm sure you've done your best to change your life for yourself and your loved ones over the months that have passed. Start looking back over your original aims for the year that's almost over because when you do so, you're bound to notice some things that didn't quite work out as you'd planned back in January. Like everything else, plans do evolve, but sometimes you find you've lost sight of the target you were aiming for, or you got distracted by other people and their plans and went off in another direction. Analyse, be honest about any mistakes you might have made and then start to make plans for a new beginning in 2015.

WHAT SHOULD YOU FOCUS ON?

This is a time to think about your dreams for your future and perhaps to wonder where they come from and which are the ones you should pursue. Some people will say these images of what could be are just fuelled by 'imagination', but what is imagination? I would say imagination is just the manifestation of the knowledge your higher self has. This means that scenarios you apparently 'imagine' could be your soul's way of sending you messages. Your nighttime dreams are even freer, because they happen while you're asleep and your subconscious has free rein, especially if they occur when you're in that magical, mystical, 'half-asleep' mode.

Your dreams can also include the plans you had before you were born into this life. And those plans may have been generated by events, lessons and unfinished business from lives that are further in the past. So, if you're having trouble achieving or even formulating your dreams, this would be a good time to undergo past life regression, because if you discover the roots of your dreams, not only will you understand if they're still right for you, but you'll find out if they are realistically achievable. You'll also get valuable clues as to how to bring them to fruition in the next year.

PLANET OF THE MONTH – JUPITER

Jupiter is the mightiest of our planets and the best one to harness the power of dreams. Its size brings you to the realization that you can create a fuller and more abundant future. It allows you to broaden your horizons, and gives you the strength to take steps towards your goals. Jupiter can help you to remove the constraints that limit your confidence in yourself to achieve.

But, possibly because Jupiter *is* so large, it is also the symbol of 'plenty'. At this time of year, Jupiter can sometimes make people 'overindulge' in both the financial and physical senses. Some people can overspend wildly, and then spend the rest of the year paying for it. They can also plant the seeds of future ill-health by partying a little too hard. So, be sure to connect to Jupiter's other aspects. For instance, despite its stormy appearance, Jupiter is also known as a planet of temperate energy. By harnessing this aspect of Jupiter, you can develop a greater acceptance of the past year and dissipate any regrets or blame for anything that went wrong. This, in turn, will help to stop you from behaving a little too crazily during all the celebrations.

The festive season is often a time we use as a placebo to relieve negative feelings. Instead, utilize Jupiter's energy to think logically and sensibly about your life and your dreams and to understand which aspirations are meant to be and which may be flights of fancy, inspired not by your higher self but perhaps by others or by the fake lifestyles seen on TV or in the media. By having the right kind of goals you have much more chance of achieving them. Before you came to this life your goals were unlikely to have incorporated becoming rich and famous, and will only have involved the evolution of your soul – this is the true goal you need to aspire to.

TINA'S STORY

I've always believed in angels since I was a child, and even saw an angel appear in my room one night while in Costa Rica. I'd just finished an energy treatment in a cabaña in the jungle and was so tired that I nodded off to sleep.

In the middle of the night I woke up and saw a beautiful man in a white robe at the head of my bed. I shook my head and stared again to see if he was real and he was still there. He had dark hair, a porcelain face and was wearing layers of white robes.

I started to scream as I realized something paranormal was happening, yet he stayed there floating above my head. Why is it we sometimes freak out when something beautiful happens? I woke my husband who said, "You've been working hours as a medium. Tell him you're not available right now." I realized right away that this was not someone needing my help – this was the gift of seeing into the angelic realm. I calmed down knowing this gorgeous man was a protector – an angel – and that I could sleep safely, knowing that someone was watching over me.

I was a news reporter and anchor for many years and so sometimes I saw some of the worst and best of humanity. In the course of that career I covered one too many plane crashes. I always say a prayer to my angels before I get on a flight because I refuse to allow my fear to make my life smaller.

I was alerted from a friend who is a psychic that Saint Cupertino is the patron saint of flying and so I carry a card with his image on whenever I fly. One night when heading back to Arizona from Hawaii we had a stop-over in Los Angeles. We were told that we would all be put on the next flight out to Tucson, which was four hours later. But I had a feeling that we weren't going home that night.

As we were standing in line to be boarded, an elegant man in uniform walked up said he would not be flying tonight. He was too tired to fly all of us to Tucson and in his conscience could not take our lives in his hands when *he was this exhausted. The people in the line were stunned. Some started complaining about what an inconvenience this was to them. But I started jumping for joy. I told the crowd, "Really... you are only worried about your schedule — this man may have just saved your life. I always pray that if I am not supposed to get on a flight I don't and this is an answer to a prayer. You have tomorrow, so be glad." I then turned to the pilot who was still trying to calm the passengers and said, "Thank you — I know angels do exist."*

ANGELS IN THE NEWS

In Denmark, brothers Gustav and Oliver, aged nine years old, had been left at home briefly while their mother ran an errand. But an electrical plug shorted out and started a fire. Instead of panicking, which would have been understandable, the boys felt they were protected somehow and they remembered being told that in a fire one must stay close to the floor. So Gustav and Oliver calmly crawled under the flames back and forth with buckets of water, with which they doused the flames until the fire was out.

ANGEL SYMBOL OF THE MONTH

At this time of year people take lots of photos of loved ones, so keep an eye out for orbs, or mist and smoke on photos that shouldn't be there. Angels will often use these light effects to let you know a loved one who has passed is back to join in the festivities.

DECEMBER 2014 *Week 49*

1 Monday

This week's angel-inspired flower is GERBERA — think of a gift for a loved one 🌼

2 Tuesday

3 Wednesday

4 Thursday

'Miracles are often small — don't miss a single one.'
Silverla StMichael

5 Friday

○ **6** Saturday

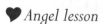 ★ *This week's angel-inspired word is UNIFORMITY*

7 Sunday

♥ *Angel lesson*

*Let your love for your angel be constant
and unfailing as theirs is for you.*

DECEMBER 2014 *Week 50*

8 Monday

9 Tuesday

This week's angel-inspired word is KNOWLEDGE ★

10 Wednesday

This week's angel-inspired flower is LILAC — remember how you felt when you were young ✿

11 Thursday

12 Friday

'Angels enlighten your life, just accept them with loving gratitude.'
Lynn Kilpatrick

13 Saturday

◐ 14 Sunday

♥ *Angel lesson*

The universe is your never-ending teacher.

DECEMBER 2014 *Week 51*

15 Monday

This week's angel-inspired word is HEAR ★

16 Tuesday

17 Wednesday

18 Thursday

This week's angel-inspired flower is THYME – look into past lives ✿

19 Friday

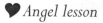 *'To make a difference where hope is lost, send angels.'*
Silverla StMichael

20 Saturday

21 Sunday

Pagan festival of Yule: the longest night of the year, recognized as the start of winter and a time when the earth rests and rebuilds. Yule also celebrates the fact that we know the sun will come again in time.

♥ *Angel lesson*

Don't close your ears to angels for fear of ridicule.

DECEMBER 2014 *Week 52*

22 Monday ●

'My steps are measured with love and light from my angels.'
Ruthie Young

23 Tuesday

24 Wednesday

This week's angel-inspired flower is RUDBECKIA — your dark
will become light ✿

25 Thursday

26 Friday

★ *This week's angel-inspired word is BRILLIANCE*

27 Saturday

◗ **28** Sunday

♥ *Angel lesson*

You are a bright, silver light shining in the darkness.

DEC 2014/JAN 2015 *Week 1*

29 Monday

....

This week's angel-inspired flower is SUNFLOWER — know no bounds

30 Tuesday

....

31 Wednesday

....

This week's angel-inspired word is PROGRESSIVENESS ★

1 Thursday

....

2 Friday

3 Saturday

💬 *'My angel, my protector = my hero.' Danni Reid*

4 Sunday

♥ *Angel lesson*
Live in the moment, but be ready to move forward.

JANUARY

M	T	W	T	F	S	S
			1	2	3	4
5	6	7	8	9	10	11
12	13	14	15	16	17	18
19	20	21	22	23	24	25
26	27	28	29	30	31	

FEBRUARY

M	T	W	T	F	S	S
						1
2	3	4	5	6	7	8
9	10	11	12	13	14	15
16	17	18	19	20	21	22
23	24	25	26	27	28	

MARCH

M	T	W	T	F	S	S
30	31					1
2	3	4	5	6	7	8
9	10	11	12	13	14	15
16	17	18	19	20	21	22
23	24	25	26	27	28	29

APRIL

M	T	W	T	F	S	S
		1	2	3	4	5
6	7	8	9	10	11	12
13	14	15	16	17	18	19
20	21	22	23	24	25	26
27	28	29	30			

MAY

M	T	W	T	F	S	S
				1	2	3
4	5	6	7	8	9	10
11	12	13	14	15	16	17
18	19	20	21	22	23	24
25	26	27	28	29	30	31

JUNE

M	T	W	T	F	S	S
1	2	3	4	5	6	7
8	9	10	11	12	13	14
15	16	17	18	19	20	21
22	23	24	25	26	27	28
29	30					

JULY

M	T	W	T	F	S	S
		1	2	3	4	5
6	7	8	9	10	11	12
13	14	15	16	17	18	19
20	21	22	23	24	25	26
27	28	29	30	31		

AUGUST

M	T	W	T	F	S	S
31					1	2
3	4	5	6	7	8	9
10	11	12	13	14	15	16
17	18	19	20	21	22	23
24	25	26	27	28	29	30

SEPTEMBER

M	T	W	T	F	S	S
	1	2	3	4	5	6
7	8	9	10	11	12	13
14	15	16	17	18	19	20
21	22	23	24	25	26	27
28	29	30				

OCTOBER

M	T	W	T	F	S	S
			1	2	3	4
5	6	7	8	9	10	11
12	13	14	15	16	17	18
19	20	21	22	23	24	25
26	27	28	29	30	31	

NOVEMBER

M	T	W	T	F	S	S
30						1
2	3	4	5	6	7	8
9	10	11	12	13	14	15
16	17	18	19	20	21	22
23	24	25	26	27	28	29

DECEMBER

M	T	W	T	F	S	S
	1	2	3	4	5	6
7	8	9	10	11	12	13
14	15	16	17	18	19	20
21	22	23	24	25	26	27
28	29	30	31			

Useful Contacts

Name:

Phone number:

Email address:

....

Name:

Phone number:

Email address:

....

Name:

Phone number:

Email address:

....

Name:

Phone number:

Email address:

....

Name:

Phone number:

Email address:

....

Name:

Phone number:

Email address:

....

Name:

Phone number:

Email address:

....

Name:

Phone number:

Email address:

....

Name:

Phone number:

Email address:

....

Name:

Phone number:

Email address:

....

Name:

Phone number:

Email address:

....

Name:

Phone number:

Email address:

....

Name:

Phone number:

Email address:

....

Name:

Phone number:

Email address:

....

Name:

Phone number:

Email address:

....

Reminders

Resources

WEBSITES

p.9: www.kiva.org – my favourite charity

p.62: www.StopSmokingStayQuit.blogspot.com – VJ's website

p.129: http://www.concettabertoldi.com/home/ – Concetta's website

p.194: www.flameofhealing.com – Freda's website

p.211: www.tinapowers.com – Tina's website

ANGEL VIDEOS

These films claim to have captured angels. I'll leave it up to you to decide if any are real.

p.48: CCTV film (http://tinyurl.com/cl6pnt2)

p.64: Kaaba film (http://tinyurl.com/cokuqeh)

p.81: Moon angel (http://tinyurl.com/c5cdwlg)

p.97: Angel of fiery light (http://tinyurl.com/bvlymdc)

p.196: Saving angel (http://tinyurl.com/8s3yyyb)

ANGELS IN THE NEWS

p.31: Brian and the 'birdies' (http://insearchofsimplicity.com/2009/10/05/the-birdies-a-father's-story/)

BOOKS

Concetta Bertoldi: *Do Dead People Watch You Shower?*
Do Dead People Walk Their Dogs? and *Inside the Other
    Side* (HarperCollins)
Bruce Van Natta: *Saved By Angels* (Destiny Image
    Publishers)
Tina Powers: *Reporting for the Other Side* (Jacquie
    Jordan Inc.)

CONTACT JENNY

Jenny would love to hear from you about your own
angel experiences. You can contact her by email,
through her website or via Facebook:
    author@globalnet.co.uk
    www.jennysmedley.com
    www.facebook.com/JennySmedleyAngelWhisperer

JOIN THE HAY HOUSE FAMILY

As the leading self-help, mind, body and spirit publisher in the UK, we'd like to welcome you to our family so that you can enjoy all the benefits our website has to offer.

EXTRACTS from a selection of your favourite author titles

COMPETITIONS, PRIZES & SPECIAL OFFERS Win extracts, money off, downloads and so much more

LISTEN to a range of radio interviews and our latest audio publications

CELEBRATE YOUR BIRTHDAY An inspiring gift will be sent your way

LATEST NEWS Keep up with the latest news from and about our authors

ATTEND OUR AUTHOR EVENTS Be the first to hear about our author events

iPHONE APPS Download your favourite app for your iPhone

HAY HOUSE INFORMATION Ask us anything, all enquiries answered

join us online at **www.hayhouse.co.uk**

Astley House, 33 Notting Hill Gate
London W11 3JQ
T: 020 3675 2450 E: info@hayhouse.co.uk

ABOUT THE AUTHOR

Tony Smedley

Jenny Smedley has had a strong connection with angels since she was a small child. Her earliest memory comes from when she was just three years old: thinking she was being separated from her mum, she jumped from a moving train and was snatched to safety by a mysterious, unseen pair of arms.

Now based in beautiful Somerset, in the UK, and happily married for over 40 years, Jenny Smedley DPLT is a qualified past-life regressionist, author, TV and radio presenter and guest, international columnist and spiritual consultant, specializing in angels and past lives. She lives with her husband, Tony, a spiritual healer, and her reincarnated 'Springador' dog, KC.

Her current life was turned around by a vision from one of her past lives, in which she knew the man known today as Garth Brooks, and problems and issues related to that life were healed and resolved in a few seconds. By following the guidance she received from her angels, she became an award-winning songwriter overnight. Her angels then helped her to overcome a lifelong phobia of flying, enabling her to go to the USA and meet Garth Brooks, so closing the circle.

For two years she hosted her own spiritual chat show on Taunton TV, interviewing people such as David Icke, Reg Presley, Uri Geller and Diana Cooper. Jenny has appeared on many TV shows in the UK, USA, Ireland and Australia, including, *The Big Breakfast* (twice), *Kelly, Open House, The Heaven and Earth Show, Kilroy* and *Jane Goldman Investigates,* as well as hundreds of radio shows, including *The Steve Wright Show* on BBC Radio 2, and *The Richard Bacon Show* on Five Live in the UK, and many in the USA, Australia, New Zealand, Iceland, Tasmania, the Caribbean, South Africa and Spain. She currently writes five columns, including for *It's Fate* and *Soul & Spirit* in the UK; *Take 5* in Australia; and *Lucky Break* in New Zealand, where she also creates digital portraits of readers' angels.